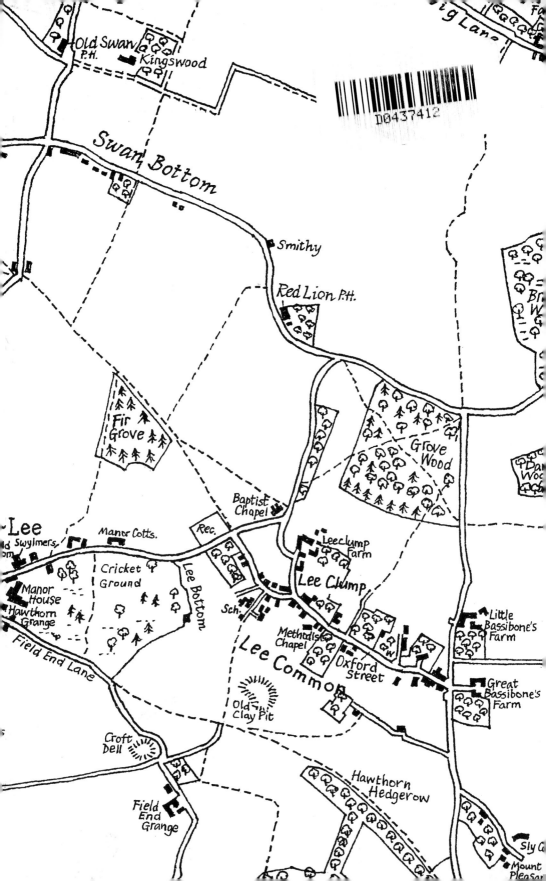

No
Finer
Courage

A Village in
the Great War

Michael Senior

SUTTON PUBLISHING

First published in the United Kingdom in 2004 by
Sutton Publishing Limited · Phoenix Mill
Thrupp · Stroud · Gloucestershire · GL5 2BU

British Library Cataloguing in Publication Data
A catalogue record for this book is available from the British Library.

ISBN 0-7509-3666-5

Front endpaper: The parish of The Lee in 1914.
Back endpaper: The area around the 2/1st Bucks, May–July 1916.

Typeset in 13/17 pt Garamond.
Typesetting and origination by
Sutton Publishing Limited.
Printed in Great Britain by
J.H. Haynes & Co., Ltd, Sparkford, England.

CONTENTS

*To the thirty men from The Lee who lost
their lives in the Great War*

In the firing line or at home, there can be no finer kind of
courage than this quietly cheerful 'carrying on' in the face of
supreme danger and difficulty. It is always great to see
people stand up to things, but when they do it in this way
one must confess to be at a loss to find words to express the
pride and gratitude one feels in them.

Walter J. Beeson, Superintendent,
Emmanuel Hall, Swan Bottom
The Lee Magazine, June 1917

ACKNOWLEDGEMENTS

I am very pleased to acknowledge the considerable help that I received in writing this book.

The Stewart-Liberty family, particularly Elizabeth Stewart-Liberty and Fenella Tillier, allowed me to use their family papers and photographs including those of Canon Constantine Phipps and G.D. Roberts and I am very much indebted to them. I would also like to thank Margaret Moffat for giving her permission to quote from W.A. Cummins's poems.

Many people from The Lee contributed documents, photographs and useful comments. Among them are Andrew Burnett, Margaret Chester, Violet Ghorst, Priscilla Gosnell, Joy Peace, Trevor Pearce, Barnaby Usborne, Denzil Walker and my companions on various trips to Fromelles – Robin Allison, Chris Carleton-Smith, Tony Kendrick, John Phimister, Richard Stewart-Liberty and Bill Waller. Margaret Richardson kindly allowed me to use extracts from The Lee Common School Log Book and the School Managers' Minute Book.

Nicholas Battle, Ian Beckett, Maureen and Andrew Blakesley, Jo and David Hamilton and Ann and Bev Risman all made valuable suggestions to improve the text.

My thanks go to the staff of the Imperial War Museum, the Public Record Office (now the National Archives), the City of Westminster Archives, the *Bayerisches Hauptstaatsarchiv (Abt. IV Kriegsarchiv)* Munich and to Roger Bettridge and his team at the Centre for Buckinghamshire Studies, Aylesbury, for their ever-patient and efficient attention. Caroline Cannon-Brookes, Richard Jeffs and the Archives Section of the Oxfordshire and Buckinghamshire Light Infantry kindly gave permission to quote extensively from the memoirs and papers of Sir Geoffry Christie-Miller.

Cheryl Mongan of Milltown Research and Publications was extremely diligent in researching material from the AWM in Canberra. Margaret Hartnell gave invaluable help translating German texts and I have benefited greatly from the input of Octave Defief, Martial Delebarre and Henri Delepierre from the Laventie–Fromelles area.

I would like to thank Jonathan Falconer, Clare Jackson, Nick Reynolds, Bow Watkinson and the staff of Sutton Publishing for their encouragement and professional help. It was a pleasure to work with them.

Finally, I want to thank my wife, Jenny, for her constant support and practical help – and for cheerfully putting up with numerous holiday 'detours' to distant parts of the Western Front.

All the above have made contributions that have significantly improved this book. Any errors are, of course, entirely mine.

Unless otherwise stated the photographs are held at the Centre for Buckinghamshire Studies, Aylesbury.

INTRODUCTION

Village war memorials are a feature of our landscape. The great majority of them were erected in the 1920s to commemorate the unprecedented number of dead of the First World War and they appear in virtually every village in Britain. They take many forms – stone crosses or monuments, bronze or marble figures, stained-glass windows, lych-gates, hospitals, gardens, village halls and clocktowers. They can be found in churches, churchyards, schools, market squares and on public buildings and village greens. Unlike the great national monuments of the Cenotaph and the Tomb of the Unknown Soldier, village war memorials are local. They were erected by local subscription and they commemorate the dead of the village regardless of rank or station. In a real sense they belong to the people and they serve, more than the memorials of any previous war, as a reminder of the sacrifice made by the community.

The war memorial in the parish of The Lee, in Buckinghamshire, stands on the village green. It takes the form of a Celtic cross made out of granite and it is inscribed with the names of the dead of two world wars. On Remembrance Sunday each year the names of the fallen are read aloud and wreaths of poppies are laid at the foot of the cross. Nine of those names are of men of The Lee who died

The Lee War Memorial was erected in 1920 and funded by local subscription.

together in July 1916 in an attack near a village in northern France called Fromelles.

This book is about that group of men and their comrades who joined the British Army in the early months of the First World War. It is about the local battalion in which they served, the attack at Fromelles and the village from which they came.

The Lee is a small parish in the Chiltern hills, 10 miles south of the county town of Aylesbury. It is made up of five hamlets – The Lee, Lee Common, Hunts Green, King's Ash and Swan Bottom. The population today is 750 – the same as it was during the First World War. In the early 1900s, about 80 per cent of the population of The Lee made their living from the land – mainly as small farmers or as labourers. Today, it is still a predominantly agricultural area, though the cottages of the tenant-farmers and the farmworkers are now more likely to house retired people or professional workers who commute to nearby towns or to London.

Some of the old families of The Lee – those who have lived in the area for generations – are still in evidence. Brown, Dwight, Keen, Monk, Pearce, Stewart-Liberty and Talmer are names that are as familiar now as they were in 1914. The name that is most associated with The Lee, however, is that of Sir Arthur Liberty. Having established a successful business in London – Liberty in Regent Street – Arthur Liberty and his wife Emma decided in 1890 to live in The Lee. He became the lord of the manor and, over a period of twenty-five years, the influence, personality and wealth of the Liberty family shaped The Lee both geographically and socially. Since the First World War there have certainly been changes in The Lee, but there is no doubt that Sir Arthur would easily recognise The Lee of today. The geographical similarities would be far more striking than the social differences.

This book has been written because there is a story to tell. In one sense the story is local – it is about the people of The Lee and about the experiences of a particular group of Lee men in the First World War. In a broader sense, however, the story is general and it is almost certainly typical of the experiences of many villages and many young soldiers of that time. The various elements of the story – the small parish, the influential lord of the manor, the local men who joined the same county battalion, and the eventual costly attack in France – will be found in many English villages. Other villages will have their own Fromelles and behind the names on the war memorials around the country will lie countless similar stories.

These stories will contain much that is individual and unique, but they will also have much in common. They will tell of those who were left at home to cope with entirely new domestic and village circumstances and of those who went away to face harrowing conditions and often death. They will tell of ordinary people who, when faced with the extraordinary events of war, behaved with outstanding determination and courage. These people must be remembered and it is for this reason that their stories must be told. What follows is one such story.

CHAPTER ONE

THE LEE BEFORE THE WAR

Where Unity and Happiness Reign
Bucks Examiner, 24 July 1914

The summer of 1914 was dry with plenty of sun. Temperatures above 100 °F were recorded on several occasions. The weather was ideal for cricket and The Lee was having an exceptional season. By the August Bank Holiday weekend, it had won nine of its twelve games and the villagers were eager to record yet another victory when, on 3 August, the Bank Holiday Monday, they played a team representing The Lee manor house. But there was talk of war – Germany had declared war on Russia two days earlier – and the minds of the cricketers were preoccupied by thoughts of mobilisation and enlistment. The match was at an interesting stage with the Manor House XI just holding its own when suddenly the weather deteriorated. Play was interrupted several times by heavy showers and at 5.00 p.m. the game was abandoned.

During one of the stoppages, three of the players, sheltering under a large tree on the edge of the ground, resolved to meet to finish the match when hostilities had ended. The three men were Ivor Stewart-Liberty, who captained the manor house team; Albert Phillips, the local fast-bowler; and G.D. 'Khaki' Roberts, an all-rounder playing for the manor house.[1] The following day, 4 August, Britain declared war on Germany. The match was never completed. All three volunteered for the Army and saw active service. Khaki Roberts survived the war unscathed. Ivor Stewart-Liberty was severely disabled and Bert Phillips was killed. Two other members of The Lee team lost their lives in the war. They were Arthur and Ralph Brown, brothers from Lee Common.

* * *

It was that August Bank Holiday weekend that marked the end of the Golden Age in The Lee. Ten days earlier, one of the local papers, the *Bucks Examiner*, had described The Lee as 'that parish which is a model of a united parish'.[2] The man behind this 'united parish' was the then squire, Sir Arthur Lasenby Liberty. Arthur Liberty, the son of a Chesham draper, had established the highly successful Regent Street store that carried his name and had become a leading figure in the world of commerce, fashion and art. He was one of the outstanding men of his generation and among his friends and supporters were the artists Whistler, Burne-Jones, Rossetti and William Morris. As an employer, Arthur Liberty was generous and considerate and he was able to inspire confidence among his staff and also among the artists and designers who worked with him. In 1890 he decided to live in The Lee as the tenant of the manor house and, in 1898, he bought the estate and became lord of the manor.

The Lee Manor *c*. 1913 – the home of Sir Arthur and Lady Emma Liberty.

The imagination and drive that had served Arthur Liberty so well in commerce was now applied to The Lee. It is as though he had some master-plan in his mind – a vision of his ideal village – and he set about shaping The Lee with characteristic vigour. He extended the manor and its estates, developed the village, enlarged the parish, and added depth and character to the social life of the locality. And he did these things in his own particular style – enlightened, autocratic, calculating, creative and with a strong leaning towards tradition and historical romanticism. Over a period of some fifteen years, Arthur Liberty altered radically both the appearance and the character of The Lee. It was a remarkable achievement that set the pattern of life in the village in his own day and influenced it to a marked extent for the next century.

In the early years of the 1900s he acquired parcels of land extending his estate from Prestwood and Wendover Dean in the west across to Arrewig Lane in the east. The estate grew in size to 3,000 acres, which included twelve farms, numerous cottages and a public house. Most of the locals had become his tenants and The Lee Manor Estate was the largest employer in the area. In 1913 the manor, in addition to its domestic staff, had forty-two estate workers, including five carpenters, nine gardeners, three gamekeepers, three chauffeurs and a coachman.[3]

Arthur Liberty was an enthusiastic developer of his estate. He extended the manor house and added an estate office, a billiard room and various outbuildings. He planted avenues of oak trees along the approach roads to the village and enclosed the manor garden with an eight-foot-high brick wall. In 1907 he altered the layout of the roads in the centre of the village, enclosing a triangular grass area and thus creating the village green. At the same time, the old eighteenth-century inn – the Cock and Rabbit – standing immediately opposite the manor house entrance, was pulled down and a new Cock and Rabbit was built on the south-west corner of the green.

Arthur Liberty – a Fellow of the Royal Historical Society and Chairman of the Bucks Architectural and Archeological Society – had a profound feeling for the past. In the early 1900s the Liberty shop had introduced the new 'Tudric' pewter and 'Cymric' silver range which reproduced Celtic and medieval designs. The Great Marlborough Street site of Liberty's was built to a Tudor design. It is not surprising,

Sir Arthur Liberty – the founder of the Liberty store in London.

therefore, that The Lee, under Arthur Liberty's careful direction, gradually developed aspects of a paternalistic 'Merrie England': a reflection of his historical and social interests. A centre for various village activities, the Guild Room, was built on the south-east corner of the green in 1897 – it stood next to Guild Cottage. The new Cock and Rabbit, the coach house at Church Farm, and various parts of the extended manor all included Tudor-style features. A parish magazine was introduced as 'a means of expressing and exchanging our views and opinions and to be a general, though local, newspaper'.[4] Parish church matters featured heavily in the magazine and the pastors and superintendents of the nonconformist chapels in Lee Common, Lee Clump and Swan Bottom were regular contributors. A public library was established in the Guild Room. The cricket club had its ground and the rifle club its range in the manor park. The football club and hockey club were provided with a sports meadow across from the church.

In 1892 Arthur Liberty introduced the annual Lee Flower Show and Sunday School Fête. The fête traditionally began with a procession of children from the school to the church for a service of thanksgiving. From there they walked to the cricket ground for the flower and vegetable show and the sports. The twenty-second anniversary of the fête, held in July 1914, was no mean affair. It was attended by the Earl and Countess of Buckinghamshire and had no fewer than twenty sports events and sixty horticultural and cookery categories. In the tug of war, The Lee and Lee Common triumphed over King's Ash and Swan Bottom 2–0.

Arthur Liberty was the moving force behind whatever happened of any significance in The Lee. He was generous with his wealth. He had water piped up to the manor house from a stream in Great Missenden and extended the supply to several houses in The Lee. In 1907 he installed the first public telephone in the village. The school in Lee Common, which had some 200 pupils, was in constant need of funds and, when it was extended in 1913, 'the Squire very kindly gave £292, besides advancing the money to meet the builder's calls without interest. And, with three other Managers, guaranteed the sum not covered by subscriptions, grants, and promises.'[5]

Over the years, Arthur Liberty had gained various official positions of authority which gave him considerable

influence. In 1894 he had been elected a district councillor
and the following year he became chairman of the newly
formed parish council – a position he held for the rest of his
life. He also became a county councillor, High Sheriff of
Buckinghamshire, Deputy Lieutenant of the County and, at
the age of seventy in 1913, he was knighted for services
to the applied and decorative arts. Within the village he was
the president of the cricket, football, rifle and hockey clubs
and of the Guild Room and Benefit Club. He was a

The Lee Hockey Club 1908–9. Arthur Brown and Ralph Brown (back
row, second and fifth from the left) are brothers from Lee Common.
(*Westminster City Archives*)

churchwarden and a school manager. His wife, Emma, also took an active part in Lee affairs as president of the Mothers' Meeting, enrolling member of the Mothers' Union and as secretary of the NSPCC.

The Libertys carried out their duties as lord and lady of the manor with zeal and commitment and they were highly regarded by the villagers. James Pearce, the Baptist pastor and a man not given to idle praise, was able to write that Arthur was 'a good landlord . . . who much improved the dwellings of the working classes' and that Lady Liberty 'was a real friend of the poor'.[6] A stained-glass window in the south transept of the village church, to the memory of Lady Liberty, shows her distributing food to a group of maimed and needy children. A visiting dignitary was able to say to the assembled villagers at the July 1914 Fête and Flower Show: 'I congratulate you all on having Sir Arthur and Lady Liberty to take care of you.'[7] Nevertheless, for most of the residents of The Lee, living conditions were basic. Water had generally to be drawn from a well. Oil lamps provided light and many villagers lived in small crowded cottages with rudimentary sanitation. The school was regularly closed because of outbreaks of measles and there were four infant deaths in the two years 1911–12.

The church registers[8] of the first decade of the century give an idea of the 'Rank and Profession' of Lee residents. The overwhelming majority – about 75 per cent – were labourers, mainly agricultural, and a further 7 per cent were directly working on the land: ploughman, gamekeeper, cowman, gardener, pheasant breeder, farmer. A number of trades were represented: bricklayer, decorator, baker, dealer, greengrocer, fruiterer, shoemaker, stone-cutter, policeman, publican, post-master, carpenter, coachman. And there was a sprinkling of professional people: clerk in holy orders, barrister, accountant, schoolmaster, dentist, an author and two 'gentlemen'.

Given this spread of occupations within The Lee, it is likely that most of the villagers lived barely above subsistence level. Their life must have been extremely simple. The gap between the great majority of the villagers and the residents of the manor house was immense. The disparity of wealth was obvious: 'a Golden Age for those who had the gold'.[9] But these were the standard conditions in rural areas at that time and, thanks to the Liberty influence, The Lee was probably one of the more socially cohesive and economically stable villages in Buckinghamshire.

* * *

One of Arthur Liberty's great talents was his ability to motivate those who worked with him. It was a talent that was evident in his commercial life in London and also in his country life in The Lee. In carrying out his numerous local projects, Arthur Liberty was able to count on the support of many capable and willing villagers. In 1914 Harry Jacobs, who lived at The Old Cottage on the green, was the Liberty estate agent, the parish church vestry clerk and the clerk to the parish council. George Lewington, who ran the post office in Lee Common, was also on the parish council and a school manager. Harry Brown, a carpenter of Lee Common,

Mr & Mrs George Lewington ran the post office in Lee Common.
George Lewington was a parish councillor and a school manager.

was a Sunday School superintendent and a member of the
churchyard maintenance committee. Ernest Young was the
headmaster of Lee Common school, a church sidesman and a
parish councillor. There were sixteen village clubs and
associations all organised by local people. The Lee was a
thriving community.

A major ally and supporter of the Squire was Canon
Constantine Phipps who, since 1895, had been vicar of St
Mary's, Aylesbury. The Libertys and the Phippses had been
friends for a number of years. Sir Arthur was patron of The
Lee church and when, in August 1914, the living became
vacant he took the opportunity to offer it to Constantine
Phipps, who readily accepted it. Phipps wrote on behalf of
his family: 'I don't think, if we had had a free choice, that we

should have selected any other village before The Lee.'[10] A new vicarage was built across the road from Church Farm and the Phipps family moved in just a few days after the outbreak of war.

For Canon Phipps, this transfer from the busy parish church of Aylesbury to the quiet backwater of The Lee was something of a step towards retirement. He was now fifty-three years of age and, after nineteen strenuous years as vicar of Aylesbury, he felt that the time had come to reduce his workload and hand over to a younger man.

The Phipps family moved from Aylesbury to The Lee in 1914 when Canon Phipps became the vicar of The Lee. Front row: Mabel and Constantine Phipps. Back row: Charles, James (Jim), Joan and Evelyn.

Constantine and Mabel Phipps had four children: James (Jim), Charles, Evelyn and Joan. Both Jim and Charles had been educated at a private school in Maidenhead and then at Winchester and, by 1914, were preparing to make their own way in life. Jim, the elder son, aged twenty-one, had already taken up a career in the Army and, after Sandhurst, had become a lieutenant in the King's (Liverpool) Regiment. Charles, aged nineteen, was less clear about his future, but had recently taken up a temporary post in Lloyds Bank in Aylesbury. The two girls, Evelyn and Joan, were both in their early twenties and were considered as charming and eligible young ladies.

Constantine Phipps was immediately appointed chairman of the school managers and quickly settled into his role as spiritual leader of the parish and confidant of the lord of the manor. Both he and his wife anticipated, with some justification, an agreeable period of quiet activity in The Lee.

* * *

If the period around the turn of the century was a Golden Age for The Lee, then 1911, the year of the coronation of George V and Queen Mary, was the *annus mirabilis*. In that year the parish church of St John the Baptist was considerably enlarged. The total cost was £3,550 of which £3,000 'was defrayed by a joint donation by the Squire and Mrs. Liberty'. Also in 1911, the Local Government Board issued an order extending the civil boundaries of The Lee to include 'the hamlets of Swan Bottom and King's Ash . . .

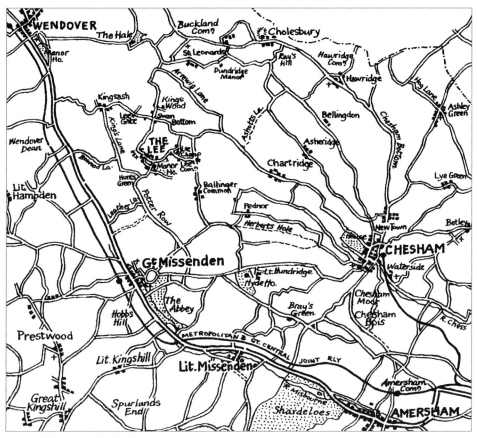

The area of The Lee in 1914.

(being all that was claimed from the Parish of Wendover) and the hamlet of Lee Common . . . of the Parish of Great Missenden'.[11]

The effect of the boundary extension was dramatic. The Lee parish acreage increased from 502 to 2,178; the size of the population increased from 125 to 775; and the number of 'inhabited houses' increased from 33 to 188. Arthur Liberty was jubilant at the outcome of this long-drawn-out tussle between the various parish councils – though the pleasure was not shared by the parishes which had ceded land. A member of the Wendover parish council, Mr F. Caudrey, 'protested against the right of certain individuals having power to acquire half a parish'. He urged the Wendover council to 'petition their Member of Parliament to bring in some Act to prevent an individual who was "in" with the County Council taking land away from a parish'.[12] The Wendover Parish Council did indeed petition their member, Mr Lionel de Rothschild, but on this particular issue it was all too late.

When the Coronation took place on 22 June, The Lee parish had much to celebrate, and Arthur Liberty and his band of helpers set about merrymaking in characteristic fashion. 'Friends and neighbours of all social ranks combined as one united family to make glad holiday.'[13] Mrs Liberty distributed Coronation mugs designed by the Squire to all the children of the parish. A special church service was arranged and this was followed by a fancy dress procession in traditional bucolic style. Over 120 villagers took part. Henry Jacobs, the Liberty estate agent, appeared as a beefeater; Ralph Brown, son of the Lee Common carpenter, was Robin Hood and Albert Phillips, the village fast-bowler, was a jester. Ironically, Harry Talmer and Albert Randall were cast as infantrymen and Arthur Bignall and Edward Witney as stretcher bearers – roles they would take up in deadly earnest some three years later.

* * *

Teulon Sonnenschien –
'Snuggins' – a regular visitor to
The Lee Weeks.

Less than two months after the Coronation celebrations, a
further outbreak of merrymaking took place: the annual Lee
Week. This was an exclusive event geared to provide
entertainment for the residents of the manor house and their
guests. The activities of The Lee Week were recorded in a
privately printed magazine. The title-sheet gives a flavour of
events: 'Ye Lee Week: A Chronicle of Merrie-Making
Holden By Youths and Maidens on Ye Chiltern Hills in Ye
Month of August 1911: Collected From Records and
Pictures Made By Themselves.' The Lee Week was simply a
great opportunity to have a good time in beautiful
surroundings – it was elitist and it was fun. Ivor Stewart, the
nephew of Arthur Liberty, had recently taken his degree at
Christ Church, Oxford and was able to invite several of his
university friends including Mark Philips, Spencer
Thomson, Teulon Sonnenschein and Khaki Roberts.

Khaki Roberts with some sporting injury.

Mark Philips and Spencer Thomson had both been at Christ Church with Ivor where they had read law together. Mark had now joined the family business while Spencer had become a solicitor in Durham. Teulon Sonnenschein had been a brilliant student at both Westminster and Christ Church, where he had met Ivor, and, after graduating, had been appointed a don at Brasenose College.

Perhaps the most flamboyant of Ivor's set was G.D. Khaki Roberts. In his autobiography, *Without My Wig*, Khaki explains how he came by his nickname: 'One summer's day in 1900, when I was 14, I fell on some gravel. I scrambled to my feet, covered with dust and a friend laughed: "You look khaki, Roberts." The name stuck.' Khaki went to school at Rugby and then went to Oxford where he read law. His main interest, however, was sport. He played cricket for his college, lawn tennis for the university, golf for Surrey and rugby for Devon, Oxford, Harlequins and England. Khaki was a genial giant of a man. He played rugby as a forward and one of his endearing habits was to ask a riddle in one scrum and answer it in the next. With his sporting prowess and sense of humour Khaki was a great favourite at The Lee Weeks.

A Lee Week group. Arthur and Emma Liberty in the centre with Khaki Roberts in front.

During The Lee Week the sun seemed always to shine and the skies were cloudless. There were cricket matches, tennis matches, bun-fights, dancing in the billiard room, and drinks on the manor house lawn. Khaki Roberts described it as 'an idyllic occasion, each day a round of one perfect pleasure after another, lawn tennis, cricket, billiards, dancing, friendship and laughter – when all the world to us was young'. One of the writers in The Lee Week *Chronicle* put it to verse:

> Now in some hammock let us respite seek
> And talk of past delight and future freak.
> Yet in our happiness let's pause awhile
> And pity those who know not a Lee Week.
>
> Here midst a friendly group beneath the bough
> A book apiece – a glass of beer – and thou
> Dear Pianola playing in the Billiard Room.
> The Cricket Week is paradise enow.

The verses were not intended to be great poetry, but they give some insight into a world of privilege and pleasure that seemed, even then, almost too good to last. Teulon Sonnenschein, in his contribution to the 1911 *Chronicle*, wrote:

> All things must end, and all good friends must part.
> Ourselves no less: but on their parent's knee
> Our children when a spouse has won our hearts
> Shall learn to lisp of Liberty and The Lee.

The Lee Week frolics with Khaki Roberts (far left), Ivor Stewart (third from the left), Mark Philips (centre) and Mary Stewart (far right).

The last Lee Week – an abbreviated version – took place at the end of July 1914.

* * *

The young men and women of the village did not have wealth or high education, but they nevertheless had their own social bonds which were just as strong as those that linked the Liberty set. They had grown up together, they had been pupils at Lee Common school together, attended church or chapel together, played games together and they often worked together. Ralph and Arthur Brown lived in

Oxford Street, Lee Common, the sons of the carpenter, Harry Brown. They had been pupils at Lee Common school and they were members of the church choir. They were keen sportsmen. Arthur played cricket and hockey and was a stalwart of the rifle club. Ralph was a member of The Lee hockey, cricket and football teams.

Both Arthur and Ralph were friends of Joe Pratt, who also lived in Oxford Street. He had left Lee Common school when he was thirteen to do what he liked doing best: work on the land. He and his brother, Harry, worked at Church Farm and later at Bassibones Farm where they were ploughmen. Across Oxford Street from the Pratts lived the Pearces. Holy Jim Pearce was the superintendent of the Lee Clump Baptist chapel and he and his wife, Sarah, lived in 'Laurel Villa' together with their eight children. Between them they ran a fruit gathering and distribution business. One of the Pearce daughters was Dora, known to all as 'Dolly'. Joe Pratt and Dolly were close friends. They had been at school together and were committed members of the Baptist congregation.

Another member of that group was Arnold Morris. Both he and Arthur Brown were employees of the manor: Arthur as a clerk in the manor estate offices while Arnold was a gamekeeper. Arnold lived along Field End Lane and, by 1914, was already married with three children. He was a quiet and capable man and, like most people in the village, he was thankful for a job that enabled him to make a living.

The young people of The Lee Weeks and those of the village lived in different worlds and they were aware of it. They did, however, have something in common that was to

Band of Hope outing from the Methodist chapel, Lee Common, *c. 1905. (Mrs Ghost)*

become of great significance. Ivor Stewart and Khaki Roberts were, within a year or so, the same age as Arthur and Ralph Brown and Arnold Morris. Charles Phipps was the same age as Joe and Harry Pratt. They had all been born in about 1890 and it was this accident of timing that ensured that these young men would share a future that had more in common than their past.

* * *

Sir Arthur and Lady Liberty had built their life in The Lee with care and considerable effort. 'It was high noon for the English country-house way of life. And Arthur Liberty had the best of both worlds, the golden commerce and the golden countryside.'[14] But the Libertys shared what must have been a major disappointment. They were unable to have children. To a man with Sir Arthur's keen sense of tradition and continuity the lack of an heir was simply unacceptable and he devised a solution to the problem with his usual businesslike determination and flair.

Sir Arthur's sister, Ada, had married an eminent Nottingham doctor, Donald Stewart, and Arthur had taken a keen interest in their second son, his godchild, Ivor. He was a bright and cheerful boy and the Libertys decided that they would finance him through Winchester and Oxford. They also encouraged him to visit the manor and take part in village activities. Ivor was a natural sportsman – he played regularly for the village cricket team – and with his ready sense of humour and attractive personality he integrated easily into the life of The Lee. Over the years, the Libertys came to regard Ivor as the son they were unable to have and the relationship was formalised in July 1913 when Ivor adopted the name 'Liberty' to become Ivor Stewart-Liberty.

Seven years earlier, Ada and Donald Stewart together with their children – Ivor, Donald, Mary and Phyllis – had moved from Nottingham to the Prebendal in Aylesbury. Here they became friendly with Canon Constantine and Mabel Phipps and the children of the two families met regularly. This had brought Ivor and Evelyn Phipps together and in June 1913 they became engaged.

On 4 October 1913 Ivor and Evelyn were married in what was one of the Buckinghamshire society weddings of the year. During the wedding celebrations Sir Arthur announced that Ivor was to be his heir. As a wedding present, Sir

Arthur built Ivor and Evelyn a substantial new house across from Pipers Field – less than half a mile from the manor house on the road to Hunts Green.

* * *

While the last, shortened Lee Week was taking place over the 1914 August Bank Holiday weekend, more serious and far-reaching events were under way on the Continent. On Bank Holiday Monday 3 August, Germany declared war on France and invaded Belgium.

Ivor Stewart-Liberty married Evelyn Phipps on 4 October 1913 at St Mary's Church, Aylesbury. Left to right: Doris Crouch, Joan Phipps, Phyllis Stewart, Mary Stewart, Betty Saunders, Anne Phipps, Evelyn Phipps, Ivor Stewart-Liberty, Jim Phipps, Spencer Thomson and Charles Phipps.

Germany's actions triggered Britain's decision to enter the war and at 11.00 p.m. on 4 August, war was declared against Germany. It was a conflict that, over the next four years, involved 57 countries and claimed the lives of over 10 million men. Of these, about 1 million were from the United Kingdom and the British Empire.[15] A war in Europe had been seen as a possibility for a number of years, but when it eventually arrived, it came as a shock.

No warnings of impending conflict had been signalled by the statesmen of Europe. Even the assassination of Archduke Franz Ferdinand of Austria-Hungary on 28 June in Sarajevo had not caused particular alarm. Most of Europe's aristocracy were doing what they usually did at that time of year: taking their holidays. The Kaiser, Wilhelm II, went yachting on the Norwegian Fjords; the German Chancellor joined a shooting party on his estates in Silesia; the Chief of the German General Staff, von Moltke, went to a spa to take the cure; Franz Joseph, the Emperor of Austria-Hungary, took his annual leave; the French President and his Prime Minister made a state visit to Russia; Sir Edward Grey, the British Foreign Secretary, went to his fishing lodge in Hampshire. More locally, the *Bucks Advertiser* of 25 July recorded that the Duchess of Buckinghamshire had left for the Continent and that Lord and Lady Wolverton had departed for Aix-les-Bains. Life seemed to be going on as normal. So, when war came, it caught Europe by surprise.

In Britain, the only war that was seriously anticipated was a war with Ireland. As one writer has summarised, 'Any reference in Britain to war in the summer of 1914 was thought to be a reference to the possibility of civil strife in Ireland, not to British involvement on the Continent.'[16] And yet, within seven days of Austria's declaration of war against Serbia – the event that signalled the start of hostilities – the Royal Navy had been mobilised and Britain was despatching its Expeditionary Force to northern France. During that short period, the countries of Europe had decided on war, had mobilised their armies and had put into effect the plans that were to determine history for the next two generations.

This lack of national awareness of impending conflict was mirrored locally. When a parliamentary by-election took place in South Bucks in February 1914 the Unionist candidate, Mr W. Baring du Pre, considered the main issues of the day to be the Constitution (the House of Lords), the Irish Question and the strength of the British Fleet. But even this last point was in the context of maintaining the glories of the British Empire rather than protecting the country from any possible German aggression.[17]

The main local newspapers of the time were the *Bucks Examiner*, which covered the Chesham and Amersham areas, and the *Bucks Advertiser* and the *Bucks Herald*, which covered the Aylesbury area. During the first half of 1914 the political contents of these papers reflected prevailing attitudes. On 9 January the *Bucks Examiner* reported an address by Canon Phipps, then at Aylesbury, as follows:

He spoke of several clouds on the horizon . . . Everybody knows that the country is face to face with matters of the utmost importance, and that these must be brought to a head within the next few months. The Vicar instanced labour unrest and dear living, the Home Rule question in Ireland, and Welsh Disestablishment, but he was very careful not to commit himself very strongly on the political side. The Country has been confronted with troubles as great as these, and has triumphantly emerged, and I don't see why 1914 should be looked forward to as a black year.

The *Bucks Examiner* of 31 July, four days before Britain declared war on Germany, presented a picture of peaceful normality. It contained notices about forthcoming events: the Tring Show, the Chartridge Sports and the Royal and Central Bucks Agricultural Show. It reported the annual meeting of Chesham Town FC and the county council meeting in Aylesbury which, it noted, 'was not productive of news of any great public interest'. In the section covering the proceedings of the petty sessions two men were summoned for drunk and disorderly behaviour in Amersham and three men appeared for failing to provide adequate lighting on their vehicles. And James Howard, an outfitter of Chesham High Street, placed an advertisement with the exhortation to readers, 'Enjoy Your Holiday'. With amazing irony, the only reference to war was in the notice for the Empire Picture Hall in Station Road, Chesham. For the three days, 3, 4 and 5 August, the lead film was entitled *The Curse of War*. It was advertised as 'a magnificent coloured drama – a picture no-one should miss. Exclusive to the Empire.' Apart from this ingenuous announcement, the

Examiner was completely silent on the subject of war until after the declaration of war itself.

In The Lee, the parish council busied itself with several discussions about the supply of water to Swan Bottom, with the introduction of a third delivery of letters in the parish and with the placing of a signpost at the top of Leather Lane.[18] The July parish magazine described the presentation made to the Revd R. Palmer, who was leaving the parish to become the rector of Princes Risborough. The Lee Clump Baptists, the Primitive Methodists in Lee Common and the chapel-goers in Swan Bottom all celebrated anniversaries of one kind or another. And war was declared.

Here was a population largely unaware of how the recent events in Europe might evolve and what the consequences might be. King George V wrote in his diary for 29 July: 'Austria has declared war on Serbia. Where will it end?' Hope was maintained, right up to the declaration of war, that peace might be preserved. Canon Phipps, preaching in Aylesbury on 2 August, said: 'I thank God that our Nation is all for a peaceful settlement of a foolish quarrel. May it please God . . . that the war clouds will pass away and the sun of peace once more shine on our distracted world.'[19]

What was about to happen in the world was completely outside normal comprehension. The state of mind of the British people was not so much evidence of complacency as an indicator of naivety. Philip Larkin ends his poem about 1914 with the line: 'Never such innocence again'.[20] Under such circumstances it is possible to forgive the *Bucks Examiner* for its headline in the 7 August edition:

The War Cloud –
Spoils the Holiday in Chesham

The deterioration in the weather that had caused the cricket match between The Lee and the Manor House to be abandoned on 3 August continued for the rest of the week. The *Bucks Examiner* ended its 7 August article on the war: 'It has been a gloomy week, and the grey skies and pouring rain have added to the gloom.'

CHAPTER TWO

THE EARLY YEARS OF
THE WAR

The War has eaten up all our little local interests.

The Lee Magazine, September 1914

The days leading up to Britain's declaration of war against Germany were a period of considerable uncertainty and confusion. The Government was understandably reluctant, and for a time unable, to arrive at a decision that would commit the country to war. The Prime Minister, Herbert Asquith, was having problems within his own party, many of whom wanted Britain to remain neutral, and the Cabinet was split. Peace rallies were taking place in London and the nation was in a state of apprehension and doubt. On 31 July 1914, the French Ambassador, Cambon, asked the British Foreign Minister, Sir Edward Grey, if England would enter the war. Grey gave a non-committal answer, pointing out that England had no commitments to France. King George V wrote in his diary on 1 August: 'Whether we shall be dragged into [the War] God only knows, but we shall not send an Expeditionary Force of the Army now. France is begging us to come to their assistance. At this moment, public opinion here is dead against us joining the War. . . .'

It was Germany's demand, on 2 August, for an un-restricted passage through Belgium into France that decided the matter. Britain had entered into a treaty in 1839 (as had Germany) to safeguard Belgium's neutrality and it was Germany's infringement of this neutrality that gave the British Government and the British people a moral basis for war.[1]

Considering the widespread doubt and confusion of the first few days of August, it is remarkable how, once the decision to go to war had been made, the people of Britain immediately adopted a unified and patriotic front. The leading article in the *Bucks Herald* (8 August) virtually repeated the speech made by Sir Edward Grey in the House of Commons five days earlier:

Our national rights are now seriously menaced, treaties and understandings with other nations . . . have been arbitrarily and contemptuously violated. And we are left with absolutely no alternative, if we wish to maintain the honour and dignity of our beloved land, but to fight side by side with nations who are also threatened . . . Happily we go into it with clean hands . . . we fight for the cause of freedom and the independence and security of the smaller nations of Europe.

These worthy sentiments became the rationale for war. The themes were developed and repeated across the country. In September 1914 the editor of *The Lee Magazine* wrote: 'English troops are ready and eager to show the teeth of the

British Lion in defence of honour and to extract revenge for the violation of a treaty of the nations.'[2]

The churches of The Lee were quick to support the cause. Canon Phipps held a special service in the parish church on 21 August on behalf of 'His Majesty's Naval and Military Forces now engaged in the War'. Walter Beeson, the superintendent of Emmanuel Hall, Swan Bottom, told his congregation: 'We cannot but believe, without a doubt, that this is a Righteous War on our part and that our Nation was compelled to take steps for our honour's, our Country's and our King's sake.' And J.G. Cushing, the Primitive Methodist minister in Lee Common, noted how everyone was prepared 'to give of their best to safeguard our shores and honour our treaties. All this without a murmur!'

Along with the vast majority of the country, the villagers of The Lee were caught up in the prevailing euphoria of patriotism. There was a mood of self-righteousness, almost relief, based on the conviction that the nation had embarked on a just and necessary war. What comment there was about the darker side of war was general and vague. James Pearce, the Lee Clump Baptist minister, wrote in the same edition of *The Lee Magazine* that 'the sword is now at work and, we fear, with terrible results'. The Lee Common Methodist minister, J.G. Cushing, acknowledged that the nation was 'now called upon to pass through dark days of trial . . . great engines of destruction are doing their deadly work with ruthless exactitude. It is all horrible in the extreme.'[3]

But it was not yet apparent just how 'horrible' the conflict was to become. The implications of the casualty lists of

James (Holy Jim) Pearce – The Lee Clump Baptist minister. *(Mrs Joy Peace)*

Mons and Le Cateau were not yet realised. Nor was it apparent how long the war would last. Most people, in Britain as well as in Germany, were of the opinion that the war would be over soon – a short sharp conflict. The popular notion was that the war would be ended by Christmas. Admiral Beatty told his wife that the whole thing would be finished before the long winter nights came on.[4] Keynes, the economist, thought the war would last about a year because by that time all the available wealth would have been used up. Sir Archibald Murray, Chief of Staff of the British Expeditionary Force, believed that, if things went well, it would last three months and, if there were problems, about eight months.[5] The entire German war strategy was based on a quick victory in the West – their plan called for Paris to be taken in thirty-nine days. The Kaiser told his departing troops that they would be home 'before the leaves had fallen off the trees'.[6] Only a few thought that the war would last indefinitely. It was Lord Kitchener who estimated three years or longer and he was considered a wild pessimist. Sir Edward Grey's reaction to Kitchener's estimate was that 'it seemed to most of us [the Cabinet] unlikely if not incredible'.[7]

The people of The Lee and district, like most others, shared the illusion of a short war. The *Bucks Examiner* of 13 November 1914 thought that the war would end in 1914 or, possibly, in 1915. Ivor Stewart-Liberty told the men of the parish that anyone who enlisted was 'providing himself an entire change of life (which almost amounts to a holiday – for it is not for a long time)'.[8]

* * *

In October 1914 the Palace Picture House in Chesham made an alteration to its programme. Just before the start of the war the manager had booked a German film and now, some ten weeks later, 'it could not be shown at any price'.[9] It was inevitable that the intense patriotic fervour in Britain would be accompanied by anti-German feelings that at times amounted to hysteria. Sir Arthur Liberty noted in *The Lee Magazine* of October 1915 that while he had been convalescing in Buxton 'an excited mob wrecked a barber's shop as his parents happen to be German, though the man himself had never set foot in Germany'.

There was an immediate outbreak of spy-mania. The London correspondent of the *Bucks Herald* wrote: 'There is a strong and growing feeling in the Metropolis that the Government are only playing with this question of foreign spies . . . The fact that thousands of Germans are still at large in London constitutes a grave danger to the community.' The solution proposed by the correspondent was to throw all suspects into a detention centre.[10]

The spy scare spread rapidly. On 14 August 1914, the *Bucks Examiner* noted that railway bridges, waterworks, reservoirs and gasworks were all under strict surveillance. Boy Scouts guarded the reservoir at Coleshill. In the same edition, a certain Mr Bendel, a hairdresser of Chesham, emphatically denied a rumour that he was of German nationality. The following week Mr Herbert Kistruck, the landlord of the White Horse public house in Chesham, wrote to the *Bucks Examiner* denying statements that he was not English. The paper added that Mr Kistruck had sent a drawing of two men resorting to fisticuffs to settle a dispute with the remark: 'I shall be pleased to prove to the persons who circulated the rumour that I am a true-born Englishman.' On the same page there was a report of an alleged spy who had been arrested in Windsor. A rumour circulated that a Zeppelin base had been found near Great Missenden.[11] Even the respectable Khaki Roberts was accused of spying by a hostile crowd in Richmond Park. This was simply because he and half-a-dozen other young army recruits, not yet in uniform, were seen carrying out a map-reading exercise.[12]

Anti-German feelings became stronger as the war went on. One of the regular pre-war visitors to The Lee manor house, Teulon Sonnenschein, experienced anti-German hostility because of his name. The saying of the time was: 'Once a German, always a German.'[13] Despite volunteering for the British Army and being able to prove several generations of residence in Britain, Teulon Sonnenschein felt obliged to adopt his paternal grandmother's maiden name of Stallybrass. In the same year, 1917, public pressure caused King George V to abolish the German titles held by members of his family. Windsor took the place of Saxe-Coburg-Gotha.

* * *

CHANGE OF NAME.

MR. WILLIAM SWAN SONNENSCHEIN (grandson of the Rev. Edward Stallybrass), MRS SWAN SONNENSCHEIN and MISS SWAN SONNENSCHEIN, of 20 Linden Gardens, W., and "High Morcote," Shalford, Surrey, MR. WILLIAM TEULON SWAN SONNENSCHEIN, of Brasenose College, Oxford, and 20 Linden Gardens, W. and LIEUTENANT EDWARD OLIVER SONNENSCHEIN, R.N. (son of Prof. E. A. SONNENSCHEIN, Litt. D. and great-grandson of the Rev. Edward Stallybrass), desire to inform their friends that they have renounced the name of Sonnenschein and assumed the name of STALLYBRASS.

21st December, 1917.

Teulon Sonnenschein was obliged to change his name in 1917 because of anti-German feeling.

While the early days of the war were characterised by expressions of patriotism and duty, it soon became apparent that lofty sentiments were not, in themselves, enough. Rhetoric needed to be reinforced with practicalities. The role of those who had left their families and joined the armed forces was clear, but what were those who remained at home to do? The Lee Common Methodist minister wrote: 'We who are at home must do something.'[14] James Pearce preached to the Lee Clump Baptists: 'All can help in this time of need, and each should undertake the duty that lies nearest.'[15] Practical action was required and The Lee was well placed to respond to the needs of the situation.

The features that had characterised The Lee during the Golden Years at the beginning of the century – effective local leadership, well-developed social institutions and a strong community spirit – were all now adapted to matters of war. Sir Arthur Liberty, supported by the Parish Council, and Canon Phipps, along with the ministers of the non-conformist Churches, represented the establishment – secular and ecclesiastical – in the parish. It was they who linked the local with the national effort and it was they who provided leadership and motivation, doing everything they could to maintain the morale of the locality. And they used to great effect that established means of communication, the parish magazine. The monthly *Lee Magazine* went into every house in the village. It spread news; it helped to mould local opinion; and it was a powerful instrument of propaganda.

Life in The Lee was certainly not 'business as usual'[16] – a phrase much used in the early months of the war. The villagers took on, sometimes reluctantly but more often willingly, a variety of patriotic duties and good works all aimed at supporting the war effort. The continuity of the social hierarchy and the involvement of the people of The Lee in the new initiatives gave the village a sense of purpose and stability as it adapted itself to the dramatically changed circumstances.

The early months of the war saw considerable activity. On 10 August 1914, less than a week after Britain's entry into the war, Sir Arthur Liberty called a meeting of the parish council in the Guild Room to decide how the village should begin its war effort. Three practical proposals were agreed. Facilities would be provided for drill and rifle-firing practice; there would be a meeting of the local farmers to discuss how the scarcity of labour might affect the gathering-in of the harvest; and the local post offices would hold all the information necessary for enlistment – thus saving the 20 mile-round journey to Aylesbury.

Two voluntary first aid detachments (Bucks 9 for men and Bucks 10 for women) had been established some time before the war as part of a national structure supporting the Territorial Force in case of foreign invasion. They now became attached to the Temporary Military Hospital in Aylesbury. Three local girls, Alice Pearce, Dorothy Gee and Ruth Batchelor, were assigned to the Aylesbury Hospital and, in June 1916, Nurse Wilson, a member of Bucks 10, went for six months' war service to France.

A local committee of the Mid-Bucks Divisional Relief Fund was set up with the purpose of relieving cases of hardship arising from the war. Collecting drums were placed in the two post offices in The Lee and Lee Common and donations were collected for the Soldiers and Sailors Families' Association. And Maj Gen Swann of Great Missenden, a veteran of Sudan and Somaliland, addressed the villagers on 'The War and the Army'.

The Lee quickly geared itself to a new way of life and as the conflict lengthened from months to years the various village institutions adjusted their activities to the needs of the war. As Canon Phipps wrote in the September 1915 edition of *The Lee Magazine*: 'Everything we do or say or pray about is tinged and permeated with considerations of war.' An early indication that business was not as usual was the arrival, in December 1914, of a training detachment of the Royal Army Medical Corps – 150 strong – who were billeted in The Lee area. They were given the use of the village green for drill purposes and the football field and the Guild Room for their leisure activities. They left The Lee in May 1915, but not before their officer, Maj McGrath, had presented a barometer, to be placed in the Guild Room, inscribed: 'As an appreciation of the kindness shown by Sir Arthur Liberty and the Inhabitants of The Lee District'. Sir Arthur reciprocated by giving each of the soldiers a booklet with the title: 'What Every Soldier Ought To Know'.[17]

In autumn 1914 a group of Belgian refugees took up residence in The Lee. When Germany invaded Belgium about a million civilians fled their country and out of those an estimated 100,000 came to Britain. Two families – the Fonteyns and the Beukelaers – came to The Lee, where they lived from November 1914 until August 1915. They were provided with rent-free cottages, the children attended Lee Common school and a Lee Belgian Refugee Fund, which amounted to £117 6s 1d during the period of their stay, covered their living expenses.

In a letter published in *The Lee Magazine* of January 1915, the two refugee families expressed their thanks:

> The inhabitants of The Lee can be assured that the Belgians will never forget these marks of sympathy and that we ask nothing better than that we will be able to receive, later on, in our dear country, all those who have contributed in such proportion to make us forget in a measure our sad condition.

In August 1915 M. Beukelaer moved to France where he found work. He was eventually joined there by his family. In November 1915 the Fonteyns moved to Chesham where they remained for the rest of the war. After the war both the Fonteyns and the Beukelaers returned safely to Belgium and corresponded regularly with their friends in The Lee.

A platoon of the Bucks Volunteer Corps, a local defence body for men outside military age, was formed with Harry Jacobs, the Liberty estate manager, as organiser. Service in the platoon was not immediately popular (three hours' drill each week), but after some pressure from Sir Arthur Liberty and Canon Phipps the numbers grew from three to forty-one between March and June 1915.

The Guild Room was not only the village meeting room, the library and the men's games and smoking room; it was also the venue for the War Working Party – eventually to be renamed as part of the Queen Mary Needlework Guild. Every Tuesday, from 2.15 p.m. to 7.15 p.m., a group of fifty ladies knitted and sewed for the men at the Front. Every few weeks they sent the results of their patriotic labours to the War Hospitals Supply Depot in Cavendish Square, London. In September 1915, for example, they sent 215 sandbags 'for immediate use at the Front' and in May 1916 the Working Party despatched '9 sets of pyjamas, 100 large limb bandages, 3 ambulance cushions, 4 flannelette bandages, 1 bundle of old linen, 36 white handkerchiefs, 26 pairs of knitted socks, 100 Gratton caps (the latest invention for keeping head dressings in position – and none too easy to make), 68 ward bags and 1 pair of mittens.' The Hospital Depot responded: 'Everything very nice and much appreciated'.[18] On another occasion, they sent '100 hospital bags – the War Office has asked for a constant supply'.[19] The Baptists at Lee Clump, calling themselves 'The Dorcas Society', supplemented this effort and met every second Wednesday in the chapel vestry 'to work garments for the soldiers and sailors'.[20] The household staff of the manor house bought the wool and knitted 102 pairs of socks, 3 scarves, 4 pairs of mittens and they had, as they put it, 'more socks in hand'.[21] The work of these ladies went on throughout the war.

The life of the parish church, St John the Baptist, and of the three nonconformist chapels was permeated by activities designed to maintain at least some normality in everyday village life. The parish church held a daily service and three

The Lee Branch of Queen Mary's Needlework Guild.
August 1914 — April 1919.

Mrs Adams	Miss Nellie Cook	Miss Edith Holloway	Miss R. Nash	Mrs Edgar Rose
„ Thomas Adams	„ Trissie Cook	„ Laura Halse	Mrs James Neck	„ Rodwell
„ Atkinson	„ P. Chapman	„ E. Higginbottam	Mrs Oliver	Miss P. Rowland
Miss Annie Adams	„ V. Coggins	„ Ethel Harding	Miss Amy Oliver	„ G. Rodwell
„ Amy Austin	„ Daddy	„ Doris Harding	„ Eva Parsons	„ Jessie Rose
„ Bessie Austin	„ Phyllis Daddy	„ Dorothy Holland	„ Dora Pearce	„ Rodwell
„ Edith Ashwell	Mrs Davies	„ Jeffray	„ Pickford	„ L. Richardson
„ Rose Brown	Miss Gwladys Davies	„ Edith Judge	„ E. Pickton	„ Reynard
„ Bertha Brown	„ Nellie Fraser	„ Phyllis Johnson	„ Mabel Pearce	„ L. Rutland
„ Lily Bignell	„ Hilda Fraser	Mrs H. Jacobs	„ Dora Pearce	„ Eva Rose
„ Lucy Bignell	„ Gazzana	Miss Kelsey	„ Alice Pearce	Nurse Rawson
„ Kate Bignell	„ Dora Green	„ Ellen Leek	„ C. Pearce	„ Stirling
„ Ruth Batchelor	„ Alice Green	„ Larner	„ Kate Pearce	Miss Struter
„ Ivy Batchelor	„ Emily Green	„ C. Livermore	„ E. Pickton	„ H. Saunders
„ Peggy Belcher	„ Jessie Green	„ K. Lipsett	„ M. Phillips	„ M. Stewart
„ Lois Blackmore	„ Nancy Gomm	Mrs Lloyd	„ G. Parsons	Mrs Sills
Mrs Ross Brown	Mrs W. Gomm	„ H. Lewington	„ N. Parsons	„ Sayer
„ Arthur Brown	„ G. Grainger	„ Ivor Stewart Liberty	Mrs Phipps	„ C. Tomlin
„ Bell	„ W. Holland	„ Charles Lacey	„ Paye	„ Turner
„ Bedford	„ Hope	„ Langford	„ Fred Pearce	Miss Terry
„ Fred Brown	„ P. Heny	„ Leach	„ R. Pearce	„ Rose Voles
„ Copplestone	„ Arthur Hearn	„ Meade	„ J. Pearce	„ Alice Wicks
„ Collins	„ Hughes	„ M. Maskell	„ A. Pearce	„ Lizzie Wilde
„ Guy Crouch	„ Hall	„ A. Morris	„ Platt	Mrs A. Witney
„ Callow	Miss Halse	Miss Moore	„ Pickrance	„ W. Witney
Miss Gladys Collins	„ Annie Horwood	„ G. Marcham	„ H. A. Phillips	„ Wicks
„ Louie Cook	„ Bertha Hedges	„ M. Marcham	„ Rowland	Nurse M. Wilson
Mrs H. Brown	Mrs W. Chandler	Mrs J. Morren	*Miss L. Gomme	*Miss R. Gomme

The School Children

Miss B. Parsons	Lily Bruton	Germaine Gorré	Dora Pearce	Lizzie Randall
Milly Ayres	Evelyn Bruton	Maud Emerton	Geoffrey Pearce	Dorothy Randall
Margaret Barrett	Elsie Chilton	Nancy Gomm	Lizzie Phillips	Winnie Randall
Connie Bignall	Kate Chandler	Louie Hatchett	Mary Picton	Kate Rodwell
Polly Brown	Ruby Croft	Gladys Hance	Dorothy Picton	Jessie Rodwell
Lily Brown	Doris Dwight	Dorothy Hance	Gladys Price	Frances Smith
Ivy Brown	M. Eynstone	L. Holloway	Ethel Randall	Annie Talmer
Ethel Brown	Amy Fletcher	Florrie James	Ivy Randall	Lily Talmer
May Brown	Dorothy Fletcher	Marjorie Pearce	Mabel Randall	Hilda Talmer
Agnes Windsor	Amy Warren	Kathleen Warren	Herbert Fletcher	

President. Lady Liberty.
Hon. Sec.. Miss Gertrude. V. Lockey.

The Lee branch of Queen Mary's Needlework Guild met in the
Guild Room every Tuesday to knit 'comforts' for the troops.
(*Westminster City Archives*)

services each Sunday. At the time there were thirteen Sunday school teachers. The chapels held services every Sunday with a full programme of visiting preachers. Regardless of denomination, the sermons and prayers were inevitably focused mainly on war issues. *The Lee Magazine* noted that from April 1915, the parish church bell 'was tolled every weekday at 12 o'clock noon, until further notice as an appeal to people to offer a brief silent prayer to Almighty God for our brave soldiers and sailors and those of our noble allies'.

During the war period the village school at Lee Common had around 200 pupils. The head was Ernest Young and it was he who had to deal with the day-to-day teaching issues that were both familiar and recurring. Staffing was a perennial headache. Education inspections had to be faced – generally with outstanding success. There were regular outbreaks of measles. Bad weather caused illness and burst pipes – heavy snow fell in every winter of the war. As with other village institutions, the school was unable to escape the war. The children were only too keen to help the local farmers whose labourers had left for military service. In recognition of this problem, the school opening times were changed each summer of the war to begin and finish one hour earlier. The children collected blackberries for the troops' jam and chestnuts for ammunition making. The Belgian refugees attended lessons; the children knitted comforts for the troops; and the flags of the allies, donated by Sir Arthur Liberty, were displayed in the school hall. The school managers placed honours boards in the school, listing the names of all past pupils who had joined the forces.

71

attendance | He said that the attendance for the month, ending 7 May, was very good, & worked out at 94 per cent. The number on the Books was 213.

Mr E. C. Streatfeild, H.M.I, had visited the School on 23 April, & said that he could not

H. Fraser | recognize Miss Hilda Fraser as a Supplementary Teacher in the Upper School

Gardens. | Three inspectors had visited the Evening School Gardens, & had seemed very pleased with this work.

Three Children had entered for the Minor Scholarships, 2 of them eleven years of age; & it was said they could try again if they failed

Prizes | He, the headmaster, had paid Messrs Nelson's bill for Books & represented by Lady Liberty on the 6th inst.. £2.

It was agreed that the Hon. Treasurer should refund this sum to Mr Young. at 7 the Managers' hands. viz £2. & £1.15.2.

Early Opening of School | The question of opening School on the 31 May at 8 a.m. instead of 9 a.m. — & closing School at 2 p.m., was debated by the managers: who decided that, if the Parents by a considerable majority agreed, the experiment should be made

The Lee Common school managers' minute book records that school would open and close one hour earlier in the summer so that the children could work in the fields. (*Lee Common School*)

But perhaps the most obvious and poignant sign of the war for the children of Lee Common school was the absence of many of their fathers and elder brothers on active service. Every child must have known someone who was at or on his way to the Front.

Some long-standing village institutions inevitably suffered as a result of the war. The twenty-third School Fête and Flower Show, due to be held in July 1915, was cancelled: 'In the present circumstances it would not be desirable to have the usual festal gathering.'[22] It was not reinstated until after the war. The rifle club continued through 1915, but suspended activities in 1916 'as all the shooting members are on active Military service'.[23] The football club decided not to enter a team in the local league in 1915 because of a shortage of players and the cricket club was disbanded in 1916.

* * *

On 5 August 1914 Lord Kitchener was appointed Secretary for War and a member of the Cabinet. Acting on his belief that the war would last several years and be won only after many costly battles on the Continent, Kitchener immediately set about raising an army of a million men. On 7 August he issued his first appeal for 100,000 volunteers. Soon afterwards, the famous poster, showing Kitchener in Field Marshal's cap with pointed finger and bristling moustache, bearing the slogan 'Your Country Needs You', appeared on hoardings throughout Britain.[24] An appeal for a second 100,000 men was made in late August. Recruits

The Lee Football Team 1909–10. Eleven of this team served in the war. Four were wounded and three were killed. Back row, left to right: A. Hearn, P. Dwight, P. Jennings, R. Brown, H. Lewington, A. Picton, E. Young. Middle row: H. Rodwell, E. Witney, A. Monk, M. Picton, J. Brown. Front row: L. Chandler, H. Dwight. *(Westminster City Archives)*

were required to be between the ages of nineteen and thirty-five, to be 5ft 3ins or taller and to have a chest measurement of at least 34ins. They could enlist at any military barracks or recruiting office.

Until 1916, and the arrival of the Military Service Act, which introduced conscription, the British Army and Navy were composed entirely of volunteers. Following the outbreak of war and Lord Kitchener's appeals there was an initial wave of national enthusiasm – men flooded to the recruiting centres. Kitchener's calls for 200,000 men in the first month of the war resulted in 300,000 men coming forward to enlist. Altogether, just under 2.5 million men volunteered for military service up to the end of 1915. Of these, 29 per cent joined in the first eight weeks of the war – an average of over 90,000 men per week.

But the war became insatiable for more and more men. A conflict that most people thought would last perhaps five or six months soon became a long-term, bitter struggle the end of which could not be seen. By November 1914, a position of stalemate had been reached on the Western Front and 1915 was, for Britain, a year of disenchantment and disillusion. The actions at Neuve Chapelle, Aubers Ridge, Loos, Ypres and Gallipoli not only produced alarming casualty figures; they showed no appreciable gain of territory or military advantage. The mood of euphoria of the early months of the war changed gradually to one of resigned determination. Canon Phipps's 1914 Christmas letter to his congregation spoke of 'the most terrible and awful war the world has ever known'.[25] A few weeks later he wrote that 'every week seems to bring home to us more and more the reality of the war . . . it is still dragging on slowly and monotonously'.[26] Sir Arthur Liberty's editorial letter in the July 1915 *Lee Magazine* said of the war: 'No human foresight can predict the day when it will end.' Harry Jennings of Swan Bottom, who was serving in the Ypres area, took a fatalistic view in his letter to Harry Jacobs: 'The war will not finish until every man is killed if trench warfare continues.'[27] The first anniversary of the war was marked by a solemn and dignified gathering of villagers in the Guild Room. They passed a resolution reaffirming their determination to see things through to a victory and sent it to the Prime Minister. The innocence of 1914, observed by Philip Larkin in his poem 'MCMXIV', had died by the end of 1915.

The arrival of conscription in early 1916 removed the element of choice for men of military age. Until that time, individuals had, at least in theory, the freedom to enlist or not to enlist as they chose. In practice, it was the very nature of the voluntary system that brought immense pressure on eligible men to enlist. The longer the war went on, the greater the pressure grew. It was intense and it was unrelenting and it came from all sides.

The success of the Kitchener slogan, 'Your Country Needs You', led the Parliamentary Recruitment Committee (PRC) to issue a range of posters with messages such as 'Go, It's Your Duty Lad!' and 'Take Up The Sword of Justice'. The PRC also published posters of a standard design with blank spaces to be filled in locally. One such poster, with a background map of France, read: 'Bucks Boys, Come Over Here. You're Wanted!' In total 160 different PRC posters were issued during the war years. They appeared in newspapers and magazines and were pasted on walls and hoardings across the country.

When Lord Kitchener appealed for his first 100,000 men, he was enthusiastically supported by an anonymous *Lee Magazine* contributor: 'Lord K. has asked for 100,000 men . . . It is not only the honour and the glory, but the duty of every man to serve his country in this way.'[28] There were also words of encouragement from Lee men who were already in the forces. In January 1915 Gnr David Pearce, serving in the Royal Field Artillery, wrote home: 'if there are any fellows who hesitate about enlisting, you might tell them that with such splendid officers, good quarters, and good food and plenty of it, with very interesting work, with quick promotion for those who deserve it, they ought not to hesitate a minute about enlisting'.[29] The PRC could not have scripted it better.

There was also much encouragement to join the local regiments. Maj Gen Swann addressed a meeting in Great Missenden on 5 November 1914 and made a forthright appeal for recruits:

> If we cannot obtain these in Bucks, we shall have to obtain them from elsewhere. We don't want our County Regiments filled with men from Birmingham or the East End of London. We don't want these men to fight in the name of Bucks. We want Bucks men to fight for Bucks and the King.[30]

There was no hesitation in involving the local women in the recruitment campaign. When Ivor Stewart-Liberty was in charge of the Army depot in Aylesbury, he wrote: 'You ladies of The Lee, make an effort to send me six good men.'[31] The ubiquitous General Swann pointed out at a meeting at The Lee: 'how the women and girls could aid by placing no obstacles in the way of those near and dear to them answering their country's call, but rather in encouraging them to do so'.[32]

Recruitment was promoted in every possible way. Exhortation and encouragement gave way, on some occasions, to reprimand and reproof. The parish magazine of January 1915 noted that recruitment figures had jumped in those coastal towns that had suffered from German bombardment and suggested that 'A Zeppelin raid might have an equally salutary effect on our inland districts.' Sir Arthur Liberty wrote: 'I don't know how, in after years, the men will feel who, without any sufficient reason, do not volunteer to defend their hearths and homes. I fear the shame of it will last their lives, although the poor fellows don't realise it now.'[33] An entry in *The Lee Magazine* of August 1915 made the sharp comment: 'Lee soldiers are not proud of their 36 unmarried neighbours of military age.' Bert Phillips, the Lee cricketer, was clearly thought to be dilatory in joining up and a single sentence was inserted into The *Lee Magazine*: 'Come on, Bert'.[34] Bert Phillips did enlist, into the 25th Cyclists Battalion of the London Regiment, and was killed by a sniper's bullet eighteen months later.

* * *

The men of The Lee, no doubt like other men across the country, enlisted for a variety of reasons: a personal sense of duty; a gesture of bravado; loyalty to friends; to escape boring or hard work; or simply because non-enlistment would mean some embarrassment or, at worst, alienation. And many who volunteered probably did so for a mixture of reasons which they would find difficult to articulate even to themselves. But, for whatever reason, the numbers show that the men of The Lee responded well to the call to serve King and Country. The honours board at Lee Common school lists 158 former pupils who served in the First World War. A Memento, signed by Sir Arthur Liberty and presented to the parents or wife of every soldier and sailor in the parish, was distributed in October 1916 to 75 homes. Eight men volunteered in the first month of the war. After six months there were 45 men in the forces and after a year there were 56. By the end of 1915 the number had risen to 69 and *The Lee Magazine* for December 1915 noted that 'Twenty-nine parcels, each containing a 1 pound Christmas pudding, 1 tin of Cocoa and Milk, 1 tin of Potted Meat, 1 tin of Cheese, 6 cubes of Oxo, a cake of Chocolate and 20 Cigarettes, were sent to the men at the Front; and 40 boxes each containing 100 Wills' Cigarettes were sent to those in England, at a total cost including postage of £14.10.6.'

Ivor Stewart-Liberty had estimated in August 1915 that there were 120 men in the village of military age (out of a total population of about 750). It is likely, therefore, that, by the end of 1915, some 60 per cent of eligible men had voluntarily answered the Call to Arms. In June 1916, by which time the number of men in the armed forces had risen to 105, Sir Arthur Liberty was able to write: 'It is very satisfactory to learn that there are but few men in our Parish who have not enlisted.'[35] Those who had not enlisted voluntarily became subject to conscription during the last two years of the war.

Conscription was introduced in January 1916 for single men and widowers and was extended in May to cover all men between the ages of eighteen and forty-one. In February 1918 the age limit was raised to fifty. With conscription came military tribunals. A tribunal was set up in each locality to deal with those men who claimed exemption from military service. Exemption or, more usually, deferment, could be granted to those individuals who were in 'essential' jobs – either industrial or agricultural – and also to conscientious objectors. Men from The Lee and district who claimed exemption were obliged to appear at the Chesham tribunal held weekly in Germain Street school.

Often, an individual was represented by his employer and this was the case in July 1916, when Harry Jacobs, Sir Arthur Liberty's agent, appealed on behalf of Leonard Bignall, a single man aged nineteen, from Lee Common. The *Bucks Examiner* reported:

> Bignall acted as a cowman and in his spare time looked after the poultry . . . The young man had worked in the estate office since he had left school . . . Sir Arthur Liberty was not anxious to keep single men, and the lad did not wish to shirk but it was hoped that the lad would be released until after the harvest.'[36]

After some deliberation, the tribunal gave a two-month period of exemption 'with the intimation that no further appeal must be made'. Leonard Bignall duly joined the Ox and Bucks Light Infantry in September 1916. He served in

France and, although severely wounded in the left hand, survived the war.

Conscription certainly presented a problem to the farmers of the district. In *The Lee Magazine* of October 1916, the Superintendent of Emmanuel Hall, Swan Bottom, W.J. Beeson, wrote: 'It is a great problem now very severely facing the farmer that if his men are taken it will be impossible for him even to plant the average number of acres of winter corn . . . the outlook for the arable and stock farmer is gloomy indeed.'

Occasionally, appeals were successful as in the case of Harold Keen, an agricultural labourer employed at King's Ash Farm. Keen had already been given an exemption in April 1916 and in May the tribunal finally agreed that the farm was understaffed and allowed the appeal. Similarly, William Judge, a farmer of Lee Common, was successful in his appeal for one of his labourers. Mr Judge told the tribunal: 'Before the war I had ten men and three boys. Now I have seven men, one boy and three old men.' He was asked:

Why distinguish and call them old men?
Because they are old men.
What do you call old men?
They are seventy and over.
Oh, that's very old.

When the tribunal accepted the appeal William Judge asked: 'What am I to do now?' He was told: 'Go back home about your business and be thankful you are keeping the man.'[37]

Tribunal appeals from conscientious objectors were relatively few. There were only 16,500 such claims across the whole of Britain during the period 1916–18, but they had a considerable interest value and the subject was highly emotive. In The Lee, for example, Canon Phipps felt strongly that 'If the war is to be carried to a satisfactory conclusion in the shortest possible time, then every man of military age must be compelled to do his bit.'[38] When appeals from conscientious objectors came before the tribunals they generally received a full coverage in the local press. The following cross-examination, typical of its kind, appeared in the *Bucks Examiner* of 4 August 1916 under the headline 'A Man Who Loves Germans'. It concerns one William H. Potter, aged thirty-four, a potato merchant of Chesham. Potter claimed that, as a believer in the Lord Jesus Christ, he could not kill and neither could he make munitions, but he was willing to do ambulance work in the Royal Army Medical Corps. The chairman began:

You state that you believe in loving your enemies. If we dismiss your case, will you still love us?
Yes.
Do you love Germans?
Yes, I do, just as much as I love an Englishman. God loves them, so surely I may do so.
You have a wife. If a German attacked your wife would you kill him?
I don't know what I might do. I know that my duty to God is to pray to him to tell me what to do and he

would tell me what to do to protect my wife.

Do you seriously suggest that with a German suffering from blood lust attacking your wife you would not attack him and kill him if needs be?

I have never been placed in such a predicament, but I have a duty to God and I must do it.

You have a duty to protect a defenceless woman – wouldn't you do it?

I should try to part them. Killing the German is quite different.

What you say is that you do not think it is your duty to kill.

I say I should not have a right to do so. What I should do I cannot say until the time comes.

The case ended with Potter being given a non-combatant's certificate.

In total, during the period from August 1914 to January 1916, 2.4 million men volunteered for military service. From February 1916, until the end of the war in November 1918, 2.5 million men were conscripted. A further 2.5 million men of military age were unfit for military service or were in reserved occupations.

* * *

The number of men who enlisted from The Lee during the war – whether as volunteers or as conscripts – clearly shows a high degree of local commitment to the war effort.

However, while the statistics relating to recruitment in The Lee give an overall view of the extent of enlistment they fail to reveal the human and personal dimension of individual family commitment and, in certain cases, sacrifice. Leah and Harry Brown of Lee Common had four sons in the Army. Mr and Mrs Jesse Dwight, also of Lee Common, had five sons on active service in 1916 and the Hearns of Swan Bottom had six sons who served in the war. George Emmerton enlisted and left behind a wife and six children.

An official parish record, dated July 1919, lists the names of those Lee men who had 'so worthily taken their part in the most stupendous enterprise ever undertaken by any nation at war'. There are 162 men listed on the record and a number of local surnames are repeated several times indicating immediate or extended family connections. The following names appear at least three times: Adams, Brown, Bignall, Collins, Dorrell, Dwight, Harding, Hearn, Jennings, Marcham, Payne, Picton, Pratt, Randall, Rodwell, Rutland, Sharp, Talmer, Witney and Wood. There are eleven Pearces listed and thirteen Chandlers.

Sir Arthur Liberty and the vicar, Canon Constantine Phipps, both of whom were well over military age, wore army uniform during the war to demonstrate their personal commitment to the cause. Their families were even more directly involved. Ivor Stewart-Liberty, Sir Arthur's nephew, who had married Evelyn Phipps in 1913, enlisted in October 1914. The Phippses' younger son, Charles, then aged nineteen, enlisted at the same time. Jim Phipps was already a regular soldier at the outbreak of the war. Budgie Cummins,

Canon Constantine Phipps in the uniform of an honorary chaplain to the 2/1st Bucks Battalion with his elder son Jim – a Regular soldier in the King's (Liverpool) Regiment.

who later married Ivor's sister Mary, joined up in 1914. The second Phipps daughter, Joan, married Guy Crouch from Aylesbury. Guy enlisted soon after war was declared. His brother, Lionel, was among the first group of Territorials to be mobilised. Harold Church, a barrister friend of the Libertys, joined the Army with Ivor and, in 1916, became a godfather to Ivor and Evelyn's second child, Arthur.

The gentry of The Lee were a tightly knit group. The links of family and marriage were reinforced by links of education and profession. The young men of the Liberty set who enlisted in 1914 and 1915 had common backgrounds. They went to public schools: Ivor Stewart-Liberty, Jim and Charles Phipps and Budgie Cummins were all Wykehamists. Khaki Roberts was at Rugby and the Crouch brothers went to Marlborough. Ivor, Khaki and Harold Church were Oxford men, as were Ivor's best man Spencer Thomson, Teulon Sonnenschein, who tried to join the British Army in 1915, but was rejected because of poor eye-sight, and Mark Philips. And most of this group – Ivor, Khaki, Harold, Budgie and Teulon Sonnenschein – had all embarked, before the war intervened, on a career in law. It was inevitable that when these young men entered the Army they all received commissions. The Stewart-Libertys, Phippses, Cumminses, Robertses and Churches became the officers while the Browns, Pratts, Pearces and Chandlers made up the NCOs and other ranks.

CHAPTER THREE

THE CALL TO ARMS

What our little parish has done.

The Lee Magazine, July 1916

Twenty-six recruiting stations had been set up in Buckinghamshire within days of the outbreak of war. Those nearest to The Lee were housed in the laundry in Wendover, the Conservative Club in Chesham, the bank in Amersham, the Cross Keys public house in Great Missenden and in Temple Square, Aylesbury. It was mainly in these centres that the local men answered the national Call to Arms and volunteered to become members of the British armed forces.

The Lee Magazine of July 1916 published for the first time a complete list of local men who had volunteered for service. There were 105 names in total: of these, 8 had joined the Navy, 2 were in the Royal Flying Corps and the remaining 95 were in the Army. These men from The Lee parish were spread widely throughout the British armed forces on an apparently random basis, the result of personal choice together with the promptings of the recruiting authorities keen to fill gaps in the various units. As might be expected, however, the regiments most favoured by these volunteers were those associated with their own county: the Oxfordshire and Buckinghamshire Light Infantry, of which the Buckinghamshire Battalion was a part, and the Royal Bucks Hussars. Of the 95 men from the Lee who were serving in the Army in July 1916, 45 were members of one or other of the county regiments and the largest single group – 27 – had enlisted in the local Territorial unit, the Bucks Battalion.

* * *

In the years leading up to 1914 the possibility of war with Germany and the consequent threat of invasion from the Continent became serious considerations for the British government. With these problems in mind, Asquith's Secretary of State for War, Haldane, initiated several major developments. The Regular Army at home was reconstituted

The Bucks Battalion, although part of the Ox and Bucks Light Infantry, was allowed to retain its county name and its own cap-badge.

as the British Expeditionary Force (BEF), made up of one cavalry and six infantry divisions – about 165,000 men – with the capability of moving quickly across the Channel. It adopted a khaki service dress and blancoed webbing and it was equipped with the new Lee Enfield rifle that was to remain the standard infantry weapon for the next forty years. In addition, Haldane established a new Territorial Force (TF).

The role of the Territorial Force was to provide home defence in the event of attack from the Continent and thus release the Expeditionary Force for foreign service. Territorials were part-time, unpaid soldiers who attended weekly training sessions in their local drill halls and took part in annual two-week camps. Frequently, friends encouraged one another to join the local Territorial Force. Local men were officered by local gentry – a combination that fostered a strong *esprit de corps* and fitted Haldane's aim of 'rooting the army in the people'. The Territorials were organised by County Associations and became part of the existing county regiment system. This new structure was a neat solution to the problems perceived in the early years of the twentieth century and it had two great merits. It provided a framework that gave the opportunity for unlimited expansion in the event of war and, with its links to the county regiments, it had the advantage of enabling men from the same locality to join an established military tradition.

While large counties could maintain several regular regiments, some sparsely populated counties were allowed to amalgamate – hence the Oxfordshire and Buckinghamshire Light Infantry. Men from Buckinghamshire, therefore, who wished to enlist in a local regular infantry regiment were obliged to join the Ox and Bucks with its depot in Oxford. The same pattern applied to Territorial battalions with the large county regiments having numerous associated Territorial units and the smaller counties having only one battalion. Buckinghamshire, for example, had just one TF battalion – the Bucks Battalion – based in Aylesbury. Rural counties also generally supported a Territorial cavalry unit and, in Buckinghamshire, this was the Bucks Hussars.

The British Army of 1914 had a further characteristic that marked it as quite different in nature from the armies of the other major European powers. Unlike France and Germany, the British Army was composed entirely of volunteers. It was a feature that provided problems for the recruiting authorities, but it was an engrained British tradition. The voluntary system lasted until 1916, by which time the losses sustained in the war made conscription inevitable.

* * *

When Lord Kitchener was appointed Secretary of State for War in August 1914 he turned his back on Haldane's Territorial Force. Kitchener dismissed the Territorials as being amateur and inadequately trained – a 'town-clerk's army' of 'week-end soldiers'. And, in some respects, Kitchener had a point. The Territorials were organised by County Associations and were not directly under the control of the War Office. Moreover, the men had signed on for a limited period of five years of home service and could only be sent abroad if they accepted what was known as the Imperial Service Obligation. Since many Territorials were family men in their thirties, they were understandably reluctant to commit themselves to foreign service and, in early 1914, only 7 per cent of them had done so.[1] Consequently, instead of basing the expansion of the British Army on the Territorial structure, Kitchener decided that his New Armies should be recruited, trained and exist as battalions of the Regular Army. They were to be known as Service battalions. In contrast to many Territorials, the men of the New Armies were mainly young and single and were obliged to serve for the duration of the war.

By the end of August 1914 the county regiments of the British Army were therefore made up of Regular, New Army (Service) and Territorial battalions and when *The Lee Magazine* of October 1914 published the names of recent recruits they were listed under those three headings. Ellis Austin, for example, was a Regular with the Royal Field Artillery; Albert Randall joined the 6th Battalion of the Ox and Bucks Light Infantry, one of Kitchener's New Army units; and Arthur Brown enlisted with the Bucks Battalion as a Territorial.

This structure was maintained in the county regiments throughout the war, and as more and more men were recruited so the number of battalions increased. The proliferation of battalions led to a somewhat bewildering identification system. The Ox and Bucks Light Infantry, which was typical of the county structure, had, by mid-1915, developed the following battalion formation. The 1st and 2nd were the original Regular battalions with a 3rd Battalion formed from the Special Reserve (ex-Militia). The 4th Battalion was a Territorial unit based in Oxford. The Bucks Battalion, also a Territorial, was a quite separate and unnumbered battalion based in Aylesbury. It was allowed, unusually, to maintain its county name and its own cap-badge. The 5th, 6th, 7th and 8th were Kitchener New Service battalions and the 9th was a New Army Reserve battalion.

G. R.

Your King and Country Need You.

ANOTHER 100,000 MEN WANTED.

Lord Kitchener is much gratified with the response already made to the Appeal for additional men for His Majesty's Regular Army.

In the grave National Emergency that now confronts the Empire he asks with renewed confidence that another 100,000 men will now come forward.

TERMS OF SERVICE.
(Extension of age limit.)

Age on enlistment, 19 to 35, Ex-Soldiers up to 45, and certain selected Ex-Non-Commissioned Officers up to 50. Height, 5 ft. 3 in. and upwards. Chest, 34 inches at least. Must be medically fit., General service for the War.

Men enlisting for the duration of the War will be able to claim their discharge, with all convenient speed, at the conclusion of the War

PAY AT ARMY RATES,

and Married Men or Widowers with Children will be accepted, and will draw Separation Allowance under Army conditions.

HOW TO JOIN.

Men wishing to join should apply in person at any Military Barrack or at any Recruiting Office. The address of the latter can be obtained from Post Offices or Labour Exchanges.

GOD SAVE THE KING!

Recruitment advertisement in *Bucks Herald*, 5 September 1914.

It can be seen that the Regular and Service battalions of the county regiments were identified by sequential numbers. The Territorials, however, developed a more complicated 'fractioned' system. Buckinghamshire supported only one Territorial unit and so, when a second-line Territorial battalion was raised it became the 2/1st with the original battalion taking the identification 1/1st (pronounced 'second-first', 'first-first', etc.). Subsequently, a 3/1st and a 4/1st came into being. When the Ox and Bucks 4th Territorial Battalion expanded, the first-line was numbered 1/4th; the second-line 2/4th; and so on.[2]

By 1918 the Ox and Bucks was made up in total of eighteen battalions spread among the brigades, divisions and corps of the armies of the BEF.[3] Of these eighteen battalions, ten had seen active service, and among them were the 1/1st and 2/1st Bucks Territorials.

* * *

The 1st Bucks Battalion, along with other Territorial units, received its orders to mobilise at 4.00 p.m. on Thursday 4 August 1914. Men from the various 1st Bucks depots – Buckingham, Chesham, High Wycombe, Marlow, Slough and Wolverton – immediately gathered and entrained for Aylesbury, the County Territorial Headquarters. According to the *Bucks Examiner*[4] the scenes 'almost beggared description. It was reminiscent of Mafeking but with a finer spirit.' The following day the 1st Bucks marched, company by company, to Aylesbury railway station. Their progress was marked 'by cheers and cheers again'. By 9.30 p.m. the crowds, who had 'swelled to enormous proportions', waved the Territorials off to their first training area: Cosham near Portsmouth.

Similar scenes of enthusiastic farewell were being repeated across Britain. By the end of the first week of August mobilisation was well advanced and the War Cabinet, after some initial confusion, had agreed the destination of the British Expeditionary Force. It was to be on the left flank of the French Army near Maubeuge in Belgium.

The regular battalions assembled and moved to their ports of embarkation – mainly Portsmouth – and thence to Le Havre or Boulogne. Considering its complexity, the whole operation went extremely smoothly. Lt Jim Phipps, son of The Lee's newly appointed vicar, was stationed in Aldershot with the 1st King's (Liverpool) Regiment. On Tuesday 4 August, he made a hurried visit home and was able to tell the *Bucks Herald* reporter that 'the men were all ready and prepared and only awaiting their orders'.[5] The orders were not long in coming. In less than two weeks from the date of mobilisation the BEF was in France. Ten days later it was marching to its appointed position on the French left when, to the surprise of both parties, it came face to face with the forward patrols of the German First Army. The action that followed took its name from a nearby mining village, Mons. During that engagement Lt Jim Phipps was wounded in the left foot. He was The Lee's first casualty.

* * *

When, on the evening of 5 August, the 1st Bucks Battalion marched from Aylesbury, they left behind a small contingent, to form a depot with its headquarters in Temple Square. The role of the depot was to attract new recruits, give them some basic training and send them on to the 1st Battalion to bring it up to strength. Recruitment went well and the *Bucks Herald* reported on 15 August that 'Recruits have come in splendidly and if other places have responded in proportion to population as well as Aylesbury, the 100,000 men asked for [by Lord Kitchener] must be more than guaranteed.' Such was the rate of enlistment that the Bucks Territorial Force Association decided on 26 September to form a Reserve Battalion.[6]

Lt Col H.M. Williams was called out of retirement in September 1914 to command the newly formed Reserve Battalion which became the 2/1st Bucks.

During September, Lt Col H.M. Williams of Wolverton, who had retired as commander of the Bucks Battalion in spring 1914, was recalled to take over the newly formed Reserve Battalion. He was soon joined by four officers transferred from the 1st Battalion on medical grounds. Among these officers was Capt Geoffry Christie-Miller, whose military service dated from 1903. Christie-Miller was blind in one eye, the result of childhood chicken-pox, and it was for this reason that he had been left behind to help Col Williams. With his extensive previous experience and commanding personality Christie-Miller soon established himself as an indispensable officer in the new Reserve Battalion. Christie-Miller later described the Aylesbury depot as being made up of '300 unruly boys, whose ages (real ages) varied between 14½ and 19 years with a few men who had joined for Home Service only'.[7]

The question of home service and the Imperial Service Obligation was a thorny one for the Territorial Force. Along with other TF units, the 1st Bucks Battalion was invited to volunteer for foreign service, and when that was put to the men on 11 August, 533 of them agreed to serve overseas while 240, including all 27 members of the band, exercised their right to be available for home service only. This was seen as something of a blow to the prestige of the 1st Battalion, whose reaction was to deprive the 240 men of their equipment, make them camp apart from the rest of the battalion, give them the nickname of 'never-dies' and send them back to Aylesbury to join the Reserve Battalion.

The band of 'D' Company of the 2/1st Bucks in 1915. Capt Ivor
Stewart-Liberty is seated in the centre.

When, in May 1915, the Reserve Battalion (by then
renamed the 2/1st) was also requested to serve abroad, 100
of the 240 men, including 26 of the 27 members of the
band, agreed to do so. Nevertheless, the high-handed actions
of the 1/1st Battalion were not forgotten and they caused
considerable and lasting friction between the two Bucks
battalions. Capt Christie-Miller wrote: 'One thing is certain,
the attitude of the 240 men had a deep effect on the
relations of the two Battalions which lasted until they met
for the first time at Albert behind the Somme line in
November 1916.' It seems, however, that the friction lasted
longer than that. After the war, each battalion set up its own
separate Old Comrades' Association and there are also
separate war memorials in St Mary's church, Aylesbury.

* * *

Lt Col Williams's main task was the training of the new recruits who were flooding into the Aylesbury depot.[8] By the end of November eight units, each of 100 men, had undergone training and some 600 men had been sent as drafts to strengthen the 1st Battalion. Lt Col Williams urgently needed additional officers to establish the 2/1st Bucks and to organise and carry out this training. He looked for them among the propertied and professional families of the county. Ivor Stewart-Liberty had already enlisted as a private in the Queen's Westminster Rifles. After six weeks' service he was offered a commission in the 2/1st Bucks. Ashley Cummins, known to his friends as 'Budgie', had been at Winchester with Ivor. He was a London barrister until 22 September when he joined the 2/1st Bucks as an officer

Lt Ashley 'Budgie' Cummins in Aylesbury, 1914.

without a single day's previous training. Charles Phipps was commissioned into the 2/1st Bucks virtually straight from Winchester. He was nineteen. His father, Canon Constantine Phipps, became an honorary chaplain to the Battalion.

Any new officer who had any military background at all was considered as something special. G.L. Stevens, who had been a sergeant in the Eton College Officer Training Corps, 'was considered such a military expert as to be able to dispense with all instruction on the Square, and after a little handling of the squad, which included rifle drill with which he was unfamiliar, was in a few days passed out by the Adjutant as a half Company commander'. Harold Church had been a sergeant in his school OTC and had also received some officer training at the Inns of Court. He was given an immediate commission and was quickly promoted. Ivor Stewart-Liberty was seen to have some natural talent for soldiering: 'so conspicuous was his aptitude for the military art and so marked his ability for handling men that before Christmas he found himself commanding a Company'.

By January 1915, Lt Col Williams had gathered together some thirty officers – the usual complement for a battalion. Among these were some Regular Army officers and some ex-Regular non-commissioned officers (NCOs). The Regulars trained the new officers and the new officers and NCOs trained the recruits. The early days in Aylesbury were hectic. The various companies were allocated training areas wherever ground was available: the cattle market, the Printers' Field, the grammar school field, the racecourse and Hartwell Park. What the officers learnt in the afternoon they taught the

Officers of the 2/1st Bucks outside their mess, the asylum cricket pavilion, in Northampton, 1915. Back row, left to right: G.C. Stevens, B.J. Newbury, R.F. Symmonds, J.M. Rolleston, J.B. Hales, R.C. Norwood, V.W. Ranger, E.M. Letts. Third row: D.G. Chadwick, W.A. Greene, G.A. Wylle, S.D. Bishop, R.T. Hughes, R.E.M. Young, C.P. Phipps, W.A. Cummins. Second row: J.E. Firminger, G.L. Troutbeck, J.G. Hubbard, H.G.S. Buckmaster, A.P. List, H. Church, G.H. Simpson, I. Stewart-Liberty. Front row: H.L.C. Barrett, D. Waller, G.T. Hankin, J.H. Hooker, Lt Col H.M. Williams, R.W. Harling, J.C. Baker, S.R. Vernon, G. Christie-Miller.

following morning. As Capt Christie-Miller put it: 'What better incentive can be found for an afternoon's instruction parade than the certainty of having to take one's place single-handed as an instructor for the whole of the next morning and face half a Company of keen-witted and critical recruits.'

Instilling discipline and order into the young recruits was no easy matter. One officer-instructor recalled training a Company of 100 (unruly) boys in the meadows of the Buckingham Road. Having closed them to march back for dinner and given them a 'Stand Easy' for five minutes I happened to turn away. On turning round again, I saw that the Company had melted away and was spread along the hedgerows picking blackberries.

Nevertheless, the commitment of the instructors and the enthusiasm of the recruits produced the desired results. Christie-Miller summed up his feelings: 'This was the foundation of the 2/1st Bucks and from this mob of children – for one can use no other word – were drawn most of the veteran Warrant Officers and N.C.O.s of 1916–18.'

Although by mid-1915 the 2/1st Bucks had received drafts from outside the county, the great majority – about 70 per cent – of this 'mob of children' had enlisted from the towns and villages of Buckinghamshire. They came from Aston Clinton, Aylesbury, Bletchley, Buckingham, Chesham, Chesham Bois, Eton, Great Missenden, Haddenham, High Wycombe, West Wycombe, Marlow, Slough, Wendover, Windsor, Wolverton, Weston Turville and Quainton. The Lee was particularly well represented – no doubt influenced by the example and encouragement of the Liberty family. The brothers Arthur and Ralph Brown of Lee Common both became sergeant-majors. Arnold Morris, the Liberty gamekeeper, qualified as a scout 1st Class. Edward Sharp of Kingswood became a corporal while Sydney Dwight of Lee Common served as a private. In 1915, this Lee contingent in the 2/1st Bucks grew. It was joined by

Harry Harding of Furze Field Lane, Percy Price from the Old Swan in Swan Bottom, Lloyd Brown, Oliver Brown, Sidney Johnson, the brothers Harry and Joseph Pratt and Albert Rutland all of Lee Common. These officers, NCOs and other ranks from The Lee trained and served in the Bucks Battalion for the rest of their war.

* * *

Soon after the 2/1st Bucks Battalion had held their first Christmas Dinner in the George Hotel, Aylesbury, there were signs that a move was imminent. A 3/1st Bucks Battalion had been formed at the end of November 1914 and in January 1915 the 2/1st received two inspections in quick succession: by Lt Gen Pole Carew and by Brig Gen the Marquess of Salisbury. On both occasions 'the turnout and steadiness on parade were commended'.[9]

On 1 February the Battalion moved to Northampton where it became part of the 184th Brigade in the 61st (South Midlands) TF Division. For sixteen months the 2/1st Bucks moved from one training location to another. After two months in Northampton the Battalion transferred to Chelmsford. In May it spent some time in Billericay and Epping, returned to Chelmsford in June and finally went in February 1916 to Parkhouse Camp on Salisbury Plain. This entire period was taken up with military training and exercises of one kind or another and, despite the transfer both in and out of several drafts of officers and men, it served to develop the Battalion into a close-knit and disciplined military unit.

Officers and non-commissioned officers of C Company, 2/1st Bucks. Capt Christie-Miller is seated in the centre of the front row and Lt Charles Phipps is second from the left.

This training period was not without incident. Moving from one set of billets to another brought its own problems. The men had been well received in the Billing area of Northampton and the officers had found themselves a comfortable mess in the cricket pavilion of the local asylum. But the move to Chelmsford in April 1915 was less convivial. The 2/1st Bucks had followed the 1/1st Bucks into the same billets in the Springfield area at a time when the local population had begun to resent the continued presence of soldiers in their homes. When eventually the 2/1st Battalion moved away in February 1916, signs were placed in windows saying 'Not available for billets' and doors were locked against army authorities anxious to find accommodation for an approaching Scottish Lowland battalion.

It was while the 2/1st Bucks were in Chelmsford that several cases of cerebro-spinal meningitis occurred. Because of a shortage of billets it had become the practice for two soldiers to share one bed and overcrowding was blamed for the outbreak. The order came that one man only should occupy one bed, but this caused even more friction with the locals since it had the effect of halving their billet money. The issue, however, resolved itself a few months later. A new draft of 350 men was sent to the Battalion in Chelmsford and the pressure on room availability quickly caused the order to be cancelled – it was back to two men per bed. When the Bucks moved to Billericay in May they were warmly received by the locals and Christie-Miller noted that

CSM Arthur Brown carrying out bayonet practice in Chelmsford, 1915.

'if ever we motored through there during the rest of the year, on a Saturday or a Sunday, a good sprinkling of Bucks could be seen visiting their old billets'.

The time at Billericay was enlivened by an outbreak of spy-mania. It was rumoured that some disguised German staff officers were at large. Road blocks were erected from Broxbourne in Hertfordshire to the Thames at South Benfleet. The 2/1st Bucks were ordered to control a 16-mile stretch from South Benfleet to Mount Nessing. Sentries were posted at road junctions and barricades were erected. All traffic was stopped and details taken. However, the exercise proved fruitless. No German officers were seen – it was said that they had escaped to the north – but the men thought it had been a great event that 'added a touch of reality to otherwise dreary schemes'.

Shortly afterwards, the Battalion was approached by several locals claiming that a certain Herr Heinrich Uberle had been seen despatching carrier-pigeons. Moreover, it was said that his house had 'concrete foundations solid enough to carry the heaviest gun'. Herr Uberle was brought to the Battalion HQ under armed guard, interrogated by the commanding officer and put in front of the local magistrates. Uberle defended himself by producing his vicar to vouch for his character and a neighbour to say that his pigeons were tame pets. He also made an impassioned plea claiming that he had demonstrated his loyalty by marrying an English girl and having six children. Eventually the case was dismissed, but when the Bucks moved from the Billericay area the same charges were again brought against

2/Lt Charles Phipps at bayonet practice, Chelmsford, 1915.

Herr Uberle, this time through a yeomanry regiment, and the process was repeated. As Christie-Miller observed, 'It was not a good time to be a German in the U.K.'

During their lengthy period of training the 2/1st Bucks were obliged to accept and release several drafts of officers and other ranks to other Bucks Battalions. Naturally, the aim of the Battalion was to keep its best soldiers and transfer only those it felt it could do without. Inevitably this caused some ill-feeling between the battalions. In June 1915 the 2/1st Battalion was ordered to send ten officers to the 1/1st Battalion, then in France. The 2/1st reported that 'there was no-one of sufficient stamp available'. But they were told to send them anyway. At about the same time the 2/1st were required to transfer two officers and fifty men to reinforce the 3/1st Battalion. This was done with great reluctance and only men of the poorest calibre were put forward. This ploy was easily recognised by the 3/1st who, when subsequently ordered to send a draft of thirty-five men to the 2/1st, sent back thirty-five of the original fifty.

In March 1916, the 2/1st Bucks experienced an unusual situation as regards troop transfers. On this occasion, the Battalion received men from a northern unit who had undertaken the Imperial Service Obligation on the understanding that they would remain in a battalion of their own regiment. They were understandably enraged when they were posted to a brigade in the South Midland Division. They had also been promised a month's leave and when this was cancelled their anger was compounded. Officers of the 2/1st Bucks, several of whom were legally qualified, helped the northerners to draft their protests which eventually reached Parliament. The month's leave was granted and Sir John French, GOC Home Forces, was sent to explain that 'nothing less than the urgency of the manpower situation would have led the War Office to have broken its word'.

The legal expertise of Capt Harold Church, a lawyer from Chesham, was evident in the case of a private in the 2/1st Bucks who had absented himself from parade. Capt Church defended the man by demonstrating that 'the Company had two separate places of parade and, as neither was specified in the orders, it could not be proved that the man was absent from the place of rendez-vous appointed by the officer'. What Harold Church did not point out was that the two places were only twenty yards apart.

Some of D Company under canvas at Epping, 1915, with Arnold Morris seated third from left.

The lengthy training programme was punctuated by occasional periods of leave. Charles Phipps kept a small pocket diary and noted on 7 May 1915 that he had been granted weekend leave and both he and Ivor Stewart-Liberty returned to The Lee from Chelmsford.[10] The following day they, together with Ivor's wife Evelyn, had a ride out in the family Rover to Marlow. Guy Crouch, who was in the 1/1st Bucks, was also on leave and he and his new wife, Joan – Charles Phipps's sister – joined them for tea.

Charles also records a period of leave in April 1916:

10 April: Start on 5 days leave. 9.45am to town. Lunch in Pagani's with Ivor, Atters, Stevens, and Cummins. Turkish Bath.

11 April: Motor to Aylesbury. Look for plovers eggs with Father. Find 4.

12 April: To Aylesbury with Ivor and Nin [Evelyn] and Susan. Lunch at the Prebendal.

13 April: Call on Crouches. Uncle Pownell arrives in afternoon. Play beanbags at Manor with Phyllis and Mary [Stewart] – great fun. Dinner at Manor.

14 April: H.C. at 9.00am. Say good-bye. Very sad. Go up to town and meet Joan. Tea with her at Elysee. Dinner at Pagani's. Stayed in Great Central Hotel.

15 April: Shop in morning. Lunch at Pagani's. Go to Zoo with Ivor. 5.30pm train to Tidworth.

For both officers and men periods of leave provided an escape to almost pre-war normality. There was, however, little normality about the wedding of Company Sgt Maj Arthur Brown and Elsie Hughes. It was a happy yet subdued affair. Arthur had known Elsie since childhood. They had both attended Lee Common school and sung together in the church choir. Elsie, who lived in Park Cottage, between The Lee and Lee Common, was well known locally. She played the organ at the parish church and was a teacher at both Lee Common school and the church Sunday school. Arthur was given leave from the Battalion in Chelmsford and the marriage took place in St John the Baptist, the village church, on 14 August. The Lee Common school Minute Book notes: 'The Chairman reported that Miss E. Hughes (Assistant Teacher) had applied for leave the 16th inst. And this was willingly granted her.' Arthur and Elsie were given a silver clock by the members of the choir and the congregation. 'Many friends attended the ceremony which,

Elsie Hughes, a teacher at Lee Common school and church organist for sixty-six years, who married Arthur Brown in August 1915. *(Mrs Gosnell)*

as most fitting in the case of a soldier going to the Front, was marked by its quietness and extreme simplicity. Mrs. Hughes, mother of the bride, gave her daughter away. There were no bridesmaids and no "best man".'[11] Their honeymoon lasted two days and on 17 August Arthur returned to his battalion and Elsie went back to school.

* * *

The reference to CSM Arthur Brown as 'a soldier going to the Front' was somewhat premature, but events were moving in that direction. The 2/1st Bucks had become a much-inspected battalion in 'a much-inspected Division'. Since leaving Aylesbury in February 1915 it had received four major inspections including one, in August 1915, by Lord

Kitchener in Hylands Park, Chelmsford. The occasion went well and, subsequently, it was claimed that 'the employment of 2nd line formations as such with the B.E.F. was finally decided upon by the authorities as a result of this inspection'.[12] This may or may not be so, but the turnout and physique of the men of the 61st Division seem to have made a favourable impression on Lord Kitchener and the Division did become the first second-line unit to be sent to France.

In anticipation of the Division going abroad, there was a final inspection by King George V on 5 May 1916 at Parkhouse Camp on Salisbury Plain. Christie-Miller described the event as 'the finest parade I have ever attended'. Charles Phipps wrote to his father: 'The King inspected us today and was introduced to all the Colonels in the Division. He told two of the Colonels that they had very fine Battalions — one was our Colonel, so we are all very

D Company NCOs at Epping, 1915, with Arthur Brown in the centre of the front row.

pleased and expect to get "free port" tonight at mess!!' Ivor
Stewart-Liberty was no less enthusiastic:

> Quite a good show yesterday – The King, Lord French,
> Sir Ian Hamilton, Lord Salisbury – they all looked
> awfully nice. The King told Bully [Lt Col Williams] he'd
> got a very smart Battalion – so everybody is pleasant and
> afterwards we did the march past – best in the Division.
> Then we cheered The King. The King saluted me quite
> nicely when I saluted him at the head of 'D' Coy.

Having impressed Lord Kitchener and the King the 2/1st
Bucks also seem to have impressed no less a body than the
canteen staff at No. 3 Parkhouse Camp. Shortly after
the Battalion had left Parkhouse, the *Bucks Herald* received
the following letter from a Mr George W. Farrow writing on
behalf of the canteen staff.

> It was our duty and pleasure to minister to the needs of
> the men of this Battalion when they were hungry and
> thirsty . . . Though the men had necessarily sometimes
> to wait a long time before their wants were supplied [the
> canteen staff] never on any occasion met with anything
> but the utmost civility and respect . . . The 2/1 Bucks
> were the most brave-hearted and cheerful set of men we
> have sent off to the Front. Honestly, there was not a
> bad'un among them. The Staff wish, in conclusion, to
> compliment the County on having presented the
> Country with such a splendid sample of men.[13]

By May 1916, the 2/1st Bucks had been in existence for some sixteen months. It had undergone basic training in Aylesbury; platoon and company exercises and musketry in Northampton; signalling, bayonet and Lewis gun instruction in Chelmsford; trench digging in Billericay; company, battalion and brigade manoeuvres in open country and wooded areas around Epping; and more musketry, bombing, trench occupation and day and night exercises on Salisbury Plain. They now felt that they had had enough of training and were eager to move abroad. The last period of training in Parkhouse Camp had been particularly intensive. Christie-Miller wrote: 'By the time the order for embarkation came the Battalion was worn out and longed to be

Dora 'Dolly' Pearce, daughter of Holy Jim Pearce, who married Joe Pratt after the war.
(*Mrs Joy Peace*)

in the line . . . to settle scores with the real enemy.' Joe
Pratt, in a letter to his girlfriend, Dolly Pearce, wrote: 'I'm
sorry that I have not had time to write to you, as we have
had plenty of work to do. We have been out nearly every
night trench-digging till ten o'clock'.[14]

During their period of training at Camp No. 3 on
Salisbury Plain, The Lee men of the 61st Division speculated
endlessly on their eventual war destination. A popular
recruiting song of the time was 'I'll Make A Man Of You'
and the 2/1st Bucks parodied the words:

> Monday we're going off to Flanders,
> Tuesday we're going off to France,
> Wednesday we smile
> When they talk about the Nile,
> Thursday the Soudan.
> Friday it's Malta or Gibraltar,
> Saturday we're going to Lahore,
> But Sunday I am willing
> To bet an even shilling
> We're here for the duration of the war.[15]

During Easter Week 1916, the time of the uprising in
Dublin, the 2/1st Bucks were ordered to be ready to move off
in a few hours – presumably to Ireland. But the hours passed
and no further orders were received. During April it gradually
became clear that the Division was destined for France. Maj
Christie-Miller, now second-in-command of the 2/1st Bucks,
went for four days (5–8 April) on what he described as a

'Cook's Tour' to learn the essentials of life at the Front. He was assigned to a battalion of the South Wales Borderers, part of the 38th (Welsh) Division, who were about to go into the line at Givenchy near Béthune. Christie-Miller spent his time making detailed notes on the essential day-to-day routines: how to take over trenches; the system for requisitioning rations and barbed wire; medical arrangements; casualty reporting procedures; the disposal of effects; how to run a court martial; the procedure for linking with the artillery and the engineers; and so on. Christie-Miller's immediate impression of the South Wales Borderers was not favourable. 'According to all outward appearances and conventional military standards their discipline was bad.'[16] But Christie-Miller had arrived direct from a home training environment. At least he noted that the SWB 'had been for four months in the trenches with very little rest and mostly in hot places in the line'. No doubt his own subsequent experiences in the trenches would have modified his judgement even further.

Charles Phipps, in a letter to his mother dated 2 May, said, 'Our Division starts going to France on Monday, so we shall go about 10 days later. It *will* be rather fun out there, I'm sure, and not such hard work as it is here.' Three days later he wrote to his father: 'It will be a bit sad leaving England, but I shall be quite happy very soon after, as I've got *such* a ripping lot of men in my Platoon. They really are *priceless* and I like them more and more every time I go out on parade.' Budgie Cummins, exercising his skills as a poet, composed the following lines a few weeks before the Battalion left for France:

We have not left our native heath
Nor dealt the Hun a blow;
Nor earned the warrior's laurel wreath,
Or grappled with the foe.

But still in mimic fight we run
Through field and wood and moor;
And spread 'neath England's sullen sun
The panoply of war.

But ah! The time at length will come
The blessed hour's at hand
When to the tune of fife and drum
We leave our native land.

Then shall the Kaiser all aquake
Spill o'er his Munich beer;
And whisper with a voice ashake
The 2nd Bucks are here.

On 14 May Capt Ivor Stewart-Liberty paid a hurried visit to The Lee. 'Reports say that he was very fit and well and he left for "over yonder" on the 15th.'[17] Ivor, together with his batman, the ex-gamekeeper Arnold Morris, crossed to France as divisional railway transport officer and in that temporary capacity met each battalion of the 61st Division as it arrived in Le Havre. This role enhanced Ivor's social life considerably: 'It was a hectic time – the officers of every battalion sought me out and said they wanted a "cheery time" before leaving for the line. My own battalion was the last to arrive.'[18]

2/1ST BUCKS. BATTALION.

Parkhouse Hats,
Salisbury.

5 May. 1916.

My darling Father.

I am so glad you are better. No one knows for certain when we are off, + when we do go we don't know where we leave England from, so it will be rather difficult for you to get down to us, but I will do my best to let you know. We shall probably leave here one night + get to Southampton or some place like that, where we shall stay in a rest camp till the next night, when we cross over. The King inspected us today + was introduced to all the Colonels in the Division. He told two of them that they had very fine Battalions — one was our Colonel, so we are all very pleased +expect to get "free port" tonight at mess!!

Jimmy seems to be having a great time getting up childrens parties + Easter egg hunts. He seems very happy + is getting on awfully well I think.

Please thank Mother for her letter + the news about Wykeham Martin + Henry Birch Reynardson.

It will be a bit sad leaving England, but I shall be quite happy very soon after, as I've got such a ripping lot of men in my Platoon. They really are priceless + I like them more + more every time I go out on parade. Best love, darling, to Mother, Nin + babes, + Aunt Hilda + Joyce — I haven't seen them for years. + dear old Uncle Percy + yourself. Your loving son. Charles.

Letter from Charles Phipps from Parkhouse Camp, 1916.

In a letter dated 24 May, Charles Phipps wrote to his mother from Parkhouse Camp: 'We are just off to Southampton and cross tonight and arrive at Le Havre at 5.00 a.m. We are *very* happy.'

CHAPTER FOUR

THE ROAD TO LAVENTIE

*Meanwhile, the war is touching us in The Lee more and
more closely.*

The Lee Magazine, July 1916

The first three months of the war saw mobilisation,
troop movements and casualty lists – all on a massive
scale. The Allies – principally France, Russia and Britain –
and the Central Powers – Germany and Austro-Hungary –
mobilised between them some 15 million men. Each of these
major powers had developed war plans designed to bring
victory within weeks. But all these plans, despite the years of
detailed attention devoted to them, came to nothing. By the
end of September 1914 it was clear that they had failed. The
Germans, following their Schlieffen Plan, made good
progress through northern France. But their armies, blooded
and delayed by the Belgians at Liège and by the British at
Mons and Le Cateau, were exhausted and their supply lines
over-extended. Moreover, poor coordination between their
First and Second Armies on the critical right wing caused
them to abandon the idea of encircling Paris. Instead, they
wheeled east exposing their flanks to the French armies
hastily gathered to defend Paris. Joffre, the French
Commander in Chief, saw the opportunity for a counter-

attack. He launched the Battle of the Marne and the Germans retreated to the Aisne. The Schlieffen Plan was abandoned.

Exhausted, the Germans decided to dig in on the high ground just north of Rheims. These trenches were intended to be temporary, but they became permanent. The French found that they were unable to make progress against these fiercely defended lines and, instead of frontal attacks, they attempted a series of outflanking movements. The Germans did the same, but each stage resulted in stalemate with the opposing armies digging-in to consolidate and strengthen their positions. This leapfrogging movement was invariably accompanied by heavy fighting and one such action developed into a month-long battle as the British defended Ypres against strong German attacks.

By early November 1914 this so-called 'race to the sea' had been completed and a line of parallel trenches stretched from the Belgian coast to the Swiss frontier – a total of some 400 miles. It became known as 'The Western Front'.

By 1916, when the 2/1st Bucks arrived in France as part of the 61st Division, the allocation of the Front among the Allied Armies had been well established. What remained of the Belgian Army held 15 miles of the line from near Nieuport to north of Ypres. The British zone stretched from Ypres, skirting the towns of Armentières, Béthune, Arras and Albert to a position just south of the Somme – a total of 80 miles. And the French held the remainder – about 300 miles. Hence, the British Army covered 20 per cent of the Western Front and it became their home for most of the remainder of

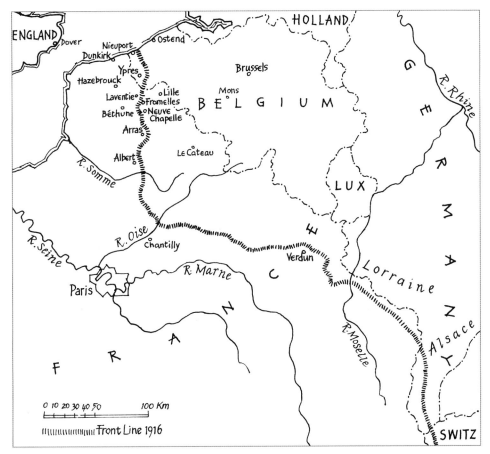

The Western Front in 1916.

the war. From November 1914 until March 1918 the line of
trenches remained virtually static. Despite their determined
efforts, neither side could gain a decisive breakthrough. One
historian summed up the situation: 'The opposing lines
congealed and grew solid. The generals on both sides stared
at these lines impotently and without understanding them.
They went on staring for nearly four years.'[1]

As far as the British were concerned, the first three months of fighting had a further outcome of major significance. Since its arrival in France in August 1914, the BEF had sustained 86,000 casualties. This represented two-thirds of its original strength. As a result of the actions at Mons, Le Cateau, the Marne and Ypres, the British Regular Army had been destroyed. 'The B.E.F. fought the Germans to a standstill, and itself out of existence.'[2] Henceforth, Britain was obliged to rely on civilian soldiers who were largely untried and untested – Kitchener's Armies, men from the Empire and the Territorials.

* * *

The 2/1st Bucks had travelled by train from Tidworth to Southampton on the afternoon of 25 May. They were given a fine send-off by the band of the 3/1st Bucks who had turned up unexpectedly at Tidworth station for that purpose. During the night they embarked on the Irish mail boat *Connaught* for Le Havre. The crossing, apparently, was far from smooth. Lt Charles Phipps who, along with the other officers, had the job of censoring letters, wrote to his brother, Jim: 'Some of these fellows writing home are damned funny. I like this kind of letter – "Just a note to say as how we got over the duck-pond safely. A lot of the boys were sick but, dear mother, I was bloody sick."' And, in a letter to his father, Charles wrote: 'One man, talking about the crossing, said – "Several were sick, but I managed to hold my own." I think that is ripping, don't you?'[3]

Before leaving for France the 61st Division allocated identification markings to all units. The Division itself adopted the Roman numerals for 61: LXI. The soldiers wore a one-inch coloured marker on each arm just below the shoulder to signify their brigade and their battalion. The men of the 2/1st Bucks wore a black circle and this identified them as members of the junior battalion of the 184th Brigade.[4] These markings were displayed on the newly issued 'tin helmets' and also on all the transport equipment. For security reasons, the practice was to cover the transport identification signs when in transit. However, as Christie-Miller pointed out, this effort at secrecy was somewhat frustrated, at least in the 2/1st Bucks, by the men constantly singing the Battalion song at the top of their voices with the last line, 'We are the Second Bucks Boys'.

On 27 May a guide led the Battalion across Le Havre to the railway station and they were soon on their way to 'a destination unknown'. In order to maintain secrecy the Battalion was informed of its route one stage at a time. The journey took twenty-two hours and the final destination was revealed only when they reached Hazebrouk, a major rail junction in northern France. They were to de-train in Berguette, a village 10 miles north-west of Béthune.

From Berguette the 2/1st Bucks marched through St Venant to their first billets in Le Sart, a hamlet just west of Merville. As they marched along the Berguette–Merville road the men became aware, for the first time, of the effects of war. Many buildings had been destroyed by shell-fire. The town hall and church at St-Venant and the cathedral at

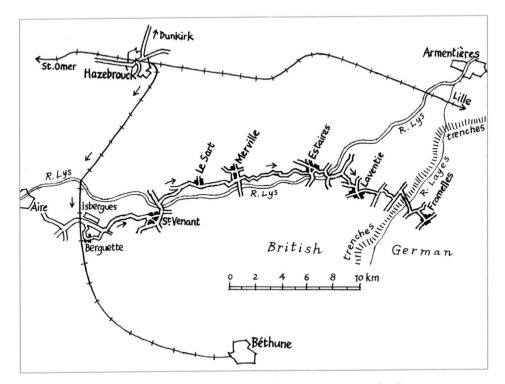

The route marched by the 2/1st Bucks from Beguette to the Front near Laventie, May 1916.

Merville had been reduced to rubble. The guns at the Front, no more than 10 miles away, could be clearly heard.

Khaki Roberts had by chance been in that same sector some nine months previously at the head of his company of the 8th Devons. He described the scenes of desolation in a letter home:

The landscape was now rather strange; houses with no roofs and in many cases without their full quota of walls

St Venant church, 1916,
destroyed by German shells.

– walls with large holes in them in addition to windows:
trees lying about the ground or standing up crookedly or
leaning against one another, and the road was decorated
with large gaping holes.[5]

In just two days the 2/1st Bucks had moved from the safe
and familiar surroundings of Parkhurst Camp on Salisbury
Plain to the battered outskirts of the war zone. The
transition was both exciting and menacing.

* * *

The following week was spent in what Christie-Miller
described as 'feverish training activity' in the Nieppe forest.
There were numerous inspections of 'gas helmets,

ammunition, rifles, field dressings, iron rations, as well as boots, kit and stores'. There was also a daily inspection for lice. Little time was allocated for recreation except for some bathing in a nearby canal. It was during one of these bathing parties that 'D' Company nearly lost Pte Townsend. Townsend, a non-swimmer, 'found himself out of his depth, but had sufficient presence of mind to walk along the bottom until he reached the side of the canal from where he was got out in a serious state'.[6]

The censorship of mail was treated as an important matter and the rules were explained at several parades. Nevertheless, there were a number of infringements – generally taking the form of some obvious codes devised to identify a nearby town or village – and these were dealt with by the Battalion officers. But few men realised that if the French postal service intercepted a letter bearing a UK address they would immediately send it to the British military authorities. One soldier was court-martialled for writing: 'I can now tell you exactly where I am as a nice little girl in Merville is posting this for me.'

On 5 June the 2/1st Bucks moved to Riez Baileul where they were inducted into the trenches by a battalion of the 38th (Welsh) Division. It was there that two companies – 'A' under Capt Harold Church and 'D' under Capt Stewart-Liberty – had their first experience of being 'in the line'. Fortunately they had a quiet time. Two days later the entire battalion was transferred to trenches in the Fauquissart sector near the town of Laventie. The method of transfer was somewhat unusual. Companies 'A' and 'D' walked down the

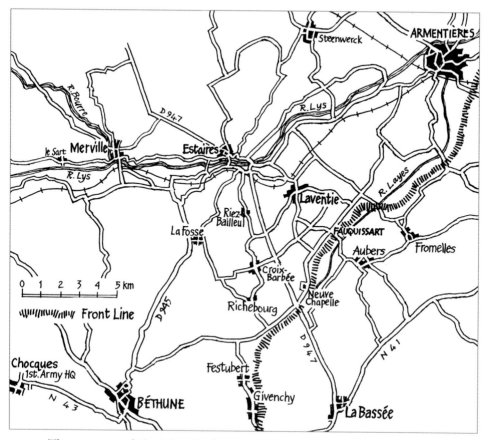

The area around the 2/1st Bucks, May–July 1916.

front line for about 2 miles in broad daylight and without
any previous reconnaissance while the remainder of the
battalion marched to the new trenches via Laventie.
Christie-Miller considered the transfer 'one of the strangest
reliefs of the war'. He then described the new position:

The front-line was a breast-work . . . with fire-bays
mostly too long. The trench consisted of duck-boards

The Town Hall, St Venant, was damaged by German shells in 1916.

but no parados. The dug-outs were sheltered with a few sheets of corrugated iron and about two rows of sandbags which would just keep out a rifle grenade but no more. The line was 1800 yds. long and posts were few and far between. Parts of the line were mined by the enemy.

Soon after entering these trenches the 2/1st Bucks had their first casualties. The Germans had put up a board saying 'Kitchener kaput'.[7] A patrol was assembled by Lt Quayle to capture the notice, but it was unsuccessful and two men were killed including Lt Quayle. At about the same time four other men were killed accidentally. One NCO (L/Cpl E.E. Jones) died while inspecting rifles; two men were killed as a result of a defective rifle grenade and one man was shot by a sentry when returning from a listening post because he failed to answer the challenge.

The particular stretch of the front-line section assigned to the 61st Division was the Fauquissart sector – from Richebourg in the south to the Red Lamp Salient, near Laventie, in the north. For the next six weeks, the 2/1st Bucks moved continuously within this sector relieving and being relieved by other units in the Division – particularly their sister battalions in the 184th Brigade, the 2/5th Glosters, the 2/4th Ox and Bucks and the 2/4th Royal Berks. The periods in the line generally lasted six days followed by six days in support and then to billets a mile or two to the rear for up to twelve days' rest – though 'rest' generally meant a series of training exercises, fatigues and inspections. During a rest period at Laventie Budgie Cummins wrote:

> Who hide behind the sandbags grey?
> And dodge the cannon balls all day,
> And in the moonbeam's misty light
> Peep out to see is Fritz all right?
> The Bucks!
>
> And then behind the line we go
> To rest, so called, a day or so,
> Which means a dozen times we trot
> The dreary trench to Masselot.[8]
> We Bucks!

Several of the rest periods were spent in or near Laventie which Christie-Miller described as 'not a wholly wrecked town, but had been a good deal knocked about. The church had been demolished . . . The town was partly inhabited and we believed that a good percentage of spies were included in the population. There were more pigeons than we liked seen flying towards the Hun line.'

But even Laventie was not entirely safe especially when the British constructed a light railway to bring a 12-in howitzer into the town. It was christened 'Laventie Liz'. When the howitzer fired 'the neighbouring houses shook – ceilings fell in; the few remaining windows broke, and retaliation [from the Germans] was immediate and accurate.' Christie-Miller's

The remains of Laventie church, 1916.

comment on this was: 'It always appeared to us that the weakest part of staff work was the allocation of rest areas for infantry in places where artillery was located. Casualties in the line cannot be prevented, but casualties that occur when artillery draws [German] fire should be avoided.'

The Fauquissart sector had been well fought-over since the beginning of the war. It had seen fierce actions during the 'race to the sea' in 1914 and since then the sector had been selected for a number of major engagements. In March 1915, FM Sir John French, the Commander in Chief of the British Army, decided to mount an attack at Neuve Chapelle – a salient jutting out into the British lines. A second and more ambitious aim of this attack was to take the Aubers Ridge. Neuve Chapelle was indeed taken by British and Indian troops, but at a tremendous cost – there were 13,000 casualties – but Aubers Ridge remained in German hands.

Aubers Ridge had a particular significance for the 2/1st Bucks and for the whole of the 61st Division. From the crest of the ridge, which stretched along the entire Fauquissart sector, the Germans had an uninterrupted view of the British lines. Months of practice had given the German artillery the opportunity to develop a high degree of accuracy when shelling the British positions – hence Christie-Miller's comments on the siting of the 12-in howitzer in Laventie.

In May 1915, only two months after the battle of Neuve Chapelle, the British and French made a further attempt to take Aubers Ridge. But the attack was doomed to fail. Since Neuve Chapelle the Germans had considerably strengthened their first- and second-line trenches with double and triple rows of barbed wire. Moreover, just behind the trenches they had prepared a defensive line of concrete bunkers each well armed with machine guns. During the battle the British, French and Indian forces lost 11,500 men. The Germans remained in possession of the Ridge and reported losses of less than 1,000.

* * *

The 61st Division had arrived in the Fauquissart sector a year after Neuve Chapelle and Aubers Ridge. By that time the area was considered reasonably quiet. It was a 'nursery' sector: a part of the line where newly arrived troops, particularly troops such as unseasoned second-line Territorials, could be initiated gradually into the rigours of trench life. When, in April 1916, Christie-Miller made his 'Cook's Tour' with the South Wales Borderers, he noted that the prevailing attitude in the trenches was 'live and let live'. His comments were critical:

> The offensive spirit must be kept up by frequent raids on enemy trenches. This keeps up men's interest and keeps them from brooding over the unpleasant situation of being shelled and mined without any personal power of retaliation. It also keeps up the idea that trenches are not for defence, but a necessary stage in the offence. The system of 'live and let live' is quite incomprehensible.'9

These comments by Christie-Miller reflect the attitude of an officer steeped in the training manuals of the time. The 'offensive' spirit was based on the belief that only continuous aggression and attack, regardless of the cost, would result in victory. At the beginning of the war the plans of all the combatants involved outright offensive. Hence the French 'attaque à l'outrage' into Alsace-Lorraine and the German advance through Belgium and northern France. In 1916, the lore of the 'offensive' still prevailed – at least in training manuals and among senior officers. The British field regulations were emphatic: 'Decisive success in battle can be gained only by vigorous offensive. Every commander who offers battle, therefore, must be prepared to assume the offensive sooner or later.' However, the results of 'offensives' were generally not encouraging. The British experiences at Mons and Le Cateau (where they were the defenders) and at Neuve Chapelle and Aubers Ridge (where they were the attackers) seemed to indicate that well-sited machine guns and even rifles, handled by determined men, could invariably hold off the most courageous attack. And it was the attackers who suffered the greater number of casualties. Nevertheless, the Germans held French and Belgian territory and threatened the Channel ports. They had to be moved and neither the British nor the French had found a suitable alternative to attack and attrition.

The Fauquissart sector may have been relatively 'quiet' for a time in early 1916, but all that had changed. The 61st Division was part of the XI Corps of the British First Army and the corps commander was Lt Gen Sir Richard Haking.

Haking was a convinced disciple of the 'offensive' and his dedication to this doctrine was to have a profound effect on the fate of the 61st Division. Earlier in his career he had taught at staff college where he had been responsible for writing the field regulations. These regulations promoted attack and aggression on every possible occasion and Haking insisted that the troops under his command should act accordingly.

Both Maj Christie-Miller and Capt Stewart-Liberty noted the occasion when they first had contact with Lt Gen Haking. Two days after the Battalion had arrived in France they were summoned to a conference in Merville. Haking lost no time in getting his message across. Stewart-Liberty wrote to his wife: 'We all went to hear the Corps Commander talk to us yesterday – he was very nice and bloodthirsty.' Christie-Miller noted:

Most of the Division officers were present . . . [Haking] outlined the military situation. The chief point in his speech was his policy on raids and great emphasis was laid on the fact that these should always originate from below and never above. The raid should be initiated by a Platoon or Company Commander based on his intimate knowledge of the line – then considered by Battalion and Brigade and sanctioned by Division.

Christie-Miller ended his notes on the Haking Conference somewhat cynically: 'We were soon to learn the difference between theory and practice.' Just two weeks later, despite

Haking's stated policy, the 61st Division Commander received an 'insistence from above that we should do a raid'. The 2/5th Glosters were selected to carry out this raid which failed miserably. Christie-Miller wrote:

> They [the Glosters] had only done one tour [in the line] and had hardly been in front of the parapet. They certainly had not that confidence in themselves and that feeling of 'ownership' of no-man's land, which is most necessary to embark on a raid with full assurance . . . No attempt at secrecy was made and details were openly discussed in Laventie . . . The date was known and I believe the time as well. When the night came the raid was met with heavy opposition. The raiding party did not reach the German lines. The Huns opened fire on the bay from which the raid was to start two minutes before Zero and disorganised the raiding party before it moved out.

On 6 July the 2/1st Bucks were sent to the Ferme du Bois area south of Fauquissart.

> This line was unpleasant since 5 days earlier the 11th and 12th Royal Sussex had been sent over in one of Haking's 'little shows' of which he was so proud. The two battalions were to take a bite out of the Boar's Head Salient and so straighten our line. Nothing was gained by this raid which resulted in between 1100 and 1200 casualties in the two battalions. Five days later some of the Royal Sussex wounded were still crawling in.

Christie-Miller commented: 'This was a truly disastrous enterprise whether we look at the effect it produced on our own troops who could only be demoralised by such handling or the effect on the enemy who could not help being elated at the use of good British troops as cannon-fodder.'

Soon after this abortive raid Christie-Miller was at the battalion headquarters in a farm on the Richebourg road. 'The association I most vividly connect with [the Head-quarters] was the Brigadier visiting our C.O. and discussing in stentorian tones in the courtyard of the farm the most secret details of a raid he had in store for us and the efforts of the C.O. to draw him into the country where his indiscretions would be less harmful.'

It was only a matter of weeks since Christie-Miller, straight from training in England, had criticised the South Wales Borderers for their 'live and let live' attitude and had recited the field regulations on the subject of the 'offence'. It had not taken long for the realities of the front line to sour his views of much of military conduct and practice.

Khaki Roberts's feelings were not dissimilar. In September 1915 he wrote:

One of the young men of the gilded staff told an illuminating story of how in one part of the line the Germans opposite threw over a conciliatory message saying they would fire high if we would do likewise. The General heard of this – said the youth mixing himself another whiskey and soda – so he went down to the trenches and made them throw bombs into the

German trenches. The result was quite a pretty little scrap – which, I gather, the General was not able to stay and watch! This is called keeping up the offensive spirit of our men.[10]

It was while the 2/1st Bucks were in the line near Ferme du Bois that The Lee contingent had their first casualties. They were Joe and Harry Pratt, the brothers from Lee Common. Ivor Stewart-Liberty wrote home on 10 July: 'Both the Pratts were wounded last night – it was a shell or

Joe Pratt of Lee Common as a prisoner of war in 1918.
(Mrs Joy Peace)

trench mortar that did it.' On 14 July he wrote: 'Harry Pratt died . . . I think he is the first of The Lee platoon to go'.[11]

* * *

During their early weeks in France Ivor Stewart-Liberty and Charles Phipps wrote frequently to their families in The Lee. The deprivation of the trenches and their natural desire to keep in touch with life back in Britain meant that their letters were often concerned with 'comforts' of one kind or another. Ivor Stewart-Liberty was particularly fortunate in having ex-gamekeeper Arnold Morris as his batman. Arnold

Harry Pratt of Oxford Street, Lee Common. He was killed on 10 July 1916 by the same shell that wounded his brother, Joe. *(Mrs Joy Peace)*

had been offered promotion on several occasions but, out of loyalty, had chosen to stay with Ivor. Shortly after he had arrived in France, Ivor wrote to his wife, Evelyn: 'Tell Mrs. Morris that Morris is splendid and looks after me like anything – such a good cook too.'

Food was important and so, apparently, were socks. As Ivor said: 'Socks is what I always want – the men too.' Charles Phipps had definite views about cigarettes: 'Abdulla cigarettes (No. 16) cost 3/8*d* a hundred out here and 6/6*d* per 100 in England – so don't send me any cigarettes.' Envelopes, on the other hand, were useful: 'Would you please send me some – thin ones . . . and mouth organs are rather good things to send out.' Both Ivor and Charles frequently received magazines from home – sometimes too many. Charles wrote to his sister, Joan: 'Will you thank Mother very much for her 2 letters and Punch and the Bystander. Don't trouble to send Punch or Bystander, please, because we had 4 Punches sent out between the six of us last week and about 6 Bystanders!! I had 2 Bystanders myself. Mother sent one and Mary [Stewart] the other.'

Receiving 'comforts' – and even writing about 'comforts' – was clearly of great importance. They were a reminder of 'normality' and trench life was far from 'normal'. The training that they had received in England could not have prepared the men of the 2/1st Bucks for this new experience which was at best filthy and uncomfortable and at worst horrific and terrifying. Almost every day they saw the dead and were themselves exposed to death or mutilation. There was constant danger from sniper-bullets, mortars and shells.

Australian troops building a trench near Armentières, 1916. Because of the high water table the trenches were constructed of sandbags to form palisades. *(IWM Q656)*

The ground that they covered was low-lying and, even in summer, often deep in slime. They had Flanders rain and, with it, Flanders mud. The landscape was flat and featureless. So-called 'rivers' were little more than drainage ditches. The low water-table, only inches below the surface, meant that trenches could not be dug deep into the ground but had to be palisades built from sandbags or, when sand was not available, from bags filled with soil or mud. And, once dug, the trenches became infested with vermin. Christie-Miller wrote: 'The smells were abominable and the line was infested with rats and mice.' It was all a far cry from the counties of the South Midlands – the home of the 61st Division – and the men from The Lee must have wondered at the contrast between their Buckinghamshire countryside and the grotesque aspect of the Fauquissart sector.

In 1915 Khaki Roberts had served at Festubert – only 2 miles south of Richebourg. In his autobiography, *Without My Wig*, written some forty years later, he recalled his experiences in that sector:

> Certainly, there was no glamour in the trenches which at marshy Festubert consisted of sandbagged breastworks. Once the thrill of being in contact with the enemy had died away and the novelty of watching shells bursting (at a safe distance) had worn off, squalor and monotony were the dominant impressions, and the indescribable stench will never be forgotten by those who sojourned in the 'old front-line'. The rats alone seemed suited to their environment: they were fat and sleek from battening on the hastily and inadequately buried corpses which at Festubert were to be found in profusion – the legacy of the battle of Aubers Ridge in the previous May.[12]

Ivor Stewart-Liberty and Charles Phipps had arrived at the Front eight months after Khaki Roberts. The conditions were no better. In their letters home Ivor and Charles wrote openly and with deep feeling about their immediate concerns – their families back in England and their abhorrence of trench life. These extracts speak for themselves.

Khaki Roberts in France.

Ivor's letters were to his wife, Evelyn, and all began with the endearment, 'Dear Nin':

18 May: If anything happens to me, carry on as you think best. Send Mowgli [Arthur] to Winchester, if possible and Oxford and let him do as he likes best, but it would be best for the family if he decided to go into Liberty's. Don't let Susan become smart or grown up before her time.

5 June: We had a service in the field yesterday and afterwards a Communion service – Charles and I and others stopped – horrid clergyman (low church – I nearly left) – rather windy – upset all the wine just as he'd blessed it. I was furious with him . . . Last night Budgie [Cummins] broke his crucifix in my room by mistake – so we are not having very good omens. We start the real thing quite soon now. Oh, darling, darling Nin I do love you so and that's the only reason I want to come out safe – and Susan and Mowgli (a bit!).

7 June: Practising gas attacks this afternoon – we're all going to be gassed for practice!!

9 June: I'm afraid there's not much in your peace idea – doesn't look like it here anyway – we and the Germans can go on like this forever, I should think.

11 June: Charles' lot lost a man last night in 'no-man's land' and the poor chap is still stuck on the wire. They'll try to get him out tonight, I expect.

12 June: I've been in these beastly trenches for 5 days now and don't know when I shall get out.

17 June: We lost our fifth officer two nights ago in my part of the front – not my Company so you don't know him – shot through the head.

20 June: It's awfully hard to be brave out here – in rat infested ditches – no enemy to look at – and always the chance of being 'done in' at any moment!

26 June: No-man's land is a horrid place – sort of valley of death – and of course it is a very difficult job to find or get a wounded or dead man out of it.

1 July: I was a fool to rush into the Infantry. They're the only people who have to go into no-man's land and make attacks. I was in too much of a hurry – the A.S.C. [Army Service Corps] was the thing – and more money. But it's rather fun and I love the men. This is a funny letter, but it's a funny place I'm in.

8 July: We've got lice now and so are proper soldiers. This isn't a very nice place – smelly – lots of dead about.

10 July: I'm within 20 yards of the Germans at one part of my line – very matey isn't it – we had a lot of shelling last night.

14 July: Came out 2 days ago – now one and a half miles back in a town without a single inhabitant or a single house with a roof on – we live in the cellar – rather a horrid desolate place. Church smashed to pieces and graves in the yard churned-up and coffins open – the French people who thought they were going to have a peaceful time because they died before the war were wrong . . . One of my sergeants had shell-shock – most unpleasant – sort of went off his head in the trenches in the middle of the night. He's getting better but won't be much use to me.

Ivor had a natural concern for his young brother-in-law, Charles Phipps, now aged twenty. He wrote to Evelyn (1 July): 'Charles was up last night – having a busy time. I hope he won't have to do anything violent – he's too young.' Charles seems never to have adapted to army life, even in England, and he found life in the trenches particularly gruelling. In November 1915, Charles had applied for a transfer to the Royal Flying Corps. His request was turned down, but in July 1916 he reapplied. On 9 July he wrote to his father: 'I have applied for a transfer to the Royal Flying Corps. It is much safer in an aeroplane than down here! I spend all my time watching them.' Charles must have discussed his plan for a transfer with Ivor who referred to it in a letter (10 July) to Evelyn: 'Charles talks about the Flying Corps – I don't know if he is going to do anything about it – he doesn't like this game too much, poor lad, nor do any of us for that matter.'

But Charles soldiered on. The entries in his pocket diary together with his letters home, express clearly his fears and his feelings:

9 June {diary}: Instruction with Welsh Regiment at Riez Bailleul. We took over the trenches without any instruction at all. We were a bit nervous but were all right after a few hours.

9 June [letter]: I have just got my steel helmet – they are very funny things. Just like Japanese hats.

10 June {diary}: March to Laventie. Occupy trenches. Shelled directly we are in. Listening patrols sent out. First time I have been under fire. One shell exploded 10 yards from me and made me very frightened for some hours.

11 June {diary}: Digging and wiring party at night. Shelled. Very nasty experience.

12 June {diary}: Fairly quiet, but I *do* hate shells.

27 June {letter}: It has been raining again and there is a horrible mess everywhere. It makes it very hard to walk about. Heaps of men are falling down in the mud all the time, cursing like anything . . . Cole was killed last week. Rotten luck, but still there are bound to be some casualties. Just going to tea now. We do have jolly good food.

27 June {diary}: In trenches. Awful mud. We go back to reserve at Laventie. Take off my clothes for first time in 18 days.

7 July {diary}: Trenches in a mess . . . many graves of unknown British soldiers. Horrible smells. Many dead in no-man's land.

Budgie Cummins expressed his feelings through his verses. While at Laventie he wrote 'The Line':

> Back again to the line. What fun!
> Just as the evening's hate's begun.
> Back to the flies and rats and dirt,
> Back to the feel of a lousy shirt . . .
> But the merry machine gun I can't stand
> With its stuttering bark over no-man's land.

Budgie followed 'The Line' with a fatalistic piece: 'Kismet':

> There are only two alternatives worth talking about here,
> And the bloke's a fool who thinks he's out to stay;
> In the one you get a blighty and return to English beer
> And the other finds you 'neath a foot of clay.

You may crawl among the retinue that hides behind the
> Staff,

You may lord it in the Royal A.S.C.

But the man with the sickle's got his eye on you not 'arf

And he'll call your hand one day as sure as T.

Long before your Mother bore you you were destined for
> the part,

And it's up to you to see that it is paid;

For the shrapnel that might burst and find a billet in your
> heart

Was for that and no other purpose made.

So you need not care a curse although you're numbered
> with the few,

Who really do the fighting in the line;

You'll not die until you're fated and you've got a job to do

And a man's job, so God help you if you whine.

In such difficult and at times terrifying circumstances Ivor took it upon himself to relieve the tension and did what he could to lift the spirits of his friends. In his letters home Charles Phipps frequently refers to Ivor's efforts:

28 May: Ivor is very well and happy and just as cheerful and funny as ever.

27 June: I had tea with Ivor the day before yesterday and I've never seen him so cheerful. There were six of us in his dugout and everyone had streaming eyes for half an hour.

28 June: [Ivor] had been sleeping all afternoon, as usual, and was very cheerful indeed and 'didn't 'arf make us larf'.

* * *

Christie-Miller records that on 12 July the 2/1st Bucks moved out of the line for a rest period in Richebourg. He described the village as: 'a scene of complete and absolute waste and desolation'. The only house left standing became

British troops in a communication trench near Laventie, 1916
(IWM Q663)

the officers' mess and the rest of the Battalion 'crashed into any hole they could find and prayed for fine weather'. The Battalion expected to be in Richebourg for five or six days, but after only two nights they received orders to move to a 'destination unknown'. The Battalion was to proceed to La Fosse and the transport section set off in that direction. One hour later new orders were received for the Battalion to move to Croix Barbe where they arrived at 6.00 a.m. on 15 July. Three hours later, just as the men were settling in, further orders came directing the Battalion to a position just north of Laventie where they arrived at 1.00 p.m.

The reason for all these orders and counter-orders became clear when they arrived at Laventie. The 61st Division, along with the 5th Australian Division, was to make an attack. Charles Phipps's diary entry for 15 July reads: 'Move to Laventie. Billetted in Farm House. Get news that we are to attack.' Ivor Stewart-Liberty wrote to his wife on 16 July: 'Looks rather exciting these days – you may not hear from me for a day or two.' The period from 16–20 July was to be the most traumatic of the war for the 61st Division and for the men of the 2/1st Bucks. Four years later Christie-Miller wrote: '[Those days] have always been a nightmare to me and always will be. I cannot attempt to describe accurately all that happened.'[13] The nightmare that he was referring to became officially known as the Attack at Fromelles. Fromelles was the name of a small town just behind the German lines across from Laventie and the attack took place on Wednesday 19 July 1916.

CHAPTER FIVE

FROMELLES –
THE PREPARATIONS

We have blundered in 1915, but here comes 1916.
Nothing it can bring can really hurt.
Revd J.G. Cushing. *The Lee Magazine*, January 1916

Two weeks before the attack at Fromelles, Ashley Budgie Cummins was ordered to attend a training course that took him away from the front line. On 1 July, Ivor Stewart-Liberty wrote to his wife and commented on Ashley Cummins's good fortune: 'Budgie – the lucky little brute – is off tomorrow on a course for a month – Boulogne – by the sea-side. Isn't he a lucky little brute? Looks like being a hard month here too – and by the sea-side.'[1] This fortuitous posting almost certainly saved Ashley Cummins's life. Had he stayed at the Front with the other Lee men of the 2/1st Bucks he would have taken part in the most wasteful and traumatic action of the Battalion's history – the attack at Fromelles. And the shattering effect of Fromelles was not limited to the 2/1st Bucks. Twelve other British and Australian battalions took part in the attack, which achieved none of its objectives and which resulted in some 9,000 men killed, wounded or taken prisoner. Just why did the attack at Fromelles take place and what made it the disaster it turned out to be?

* * *

At the beginning of 1916 there was an air of optimism among the Allied leaders. The military commanders of the four major powers – France, Britain, Russia and Italy – had met in December 1915 at Gen Joffre's lavish headquarters at Chantilly to discuss their strategy for the coming year. It was their first effort at joint planning since the beginning of the war and they agreed that they would launch major attacks simultaneously on each of their respective fronts with the aim of crippling the German and Austrian Armies. On 14 February 1916, Gen Joffre and the newly appointed British Commander in Chief, Sir Douglas Haig, met again at Chantilly to coordinate their plans for the Western Front. Haig's inclination was to attack through Flanders and threaten the important German rail centre of Lille, but Joffre insisted that a joint offensive should take place on the Somme – where the two armies could fight 'shoulder to shoulder'. Haig, under political pressure from London to support the French, reluctantly accepted Joffre's proposal. The French would provide forty divisions and the British twenty-five along a 30-mile front. Their objective was to make a decisive breakthrough on the Western Front.

However, within a week of the Joffre–Haig meeting, the Allied plans were thrown into considerable confusion. On 21 February, the Germans launched a massive and sustained assault on the French citadel of Verdun. With this one blow, the Germans gained the strategic initiative. It was Verdun, not the Chantilly Conferences, that shaped events on the Western Front in 1916.

The Germans followed up their bombardment of Verdun with a fierce infantry assault and made immediate gains. On 25 February they took Fort Douaumont. The French poured in reinforcements. The fighting grew increasingly bitter and Verdun became a slaughterhouse. By the end of March the French had lost 89,000 men and the Germans 81,000. By mid-June casualties had exceeded 200,000 on each side. By the end of the battle, in December, total French–German losses had reached 700,000. French soldiers described the battle as 'the Hell of Verdun' and as the 'mincing machine'. Nevertheless, after seven months of carnage, the city remained in French hands.

On 26 May 1916, at a stage in the Verdun battle when the French were at crisis point, Sir Douglas Haig received a visit from Gen Joffre at the British headquarters in Montreuil-sur-Mer. Joffre was in a tense mood. Haig recorded the meeting in his diary:

Joffre came straight to the point. The French had supported for three months alone the whole weight of the German attack at Verdun. Their losses have been heavy. By the end of the month they would reach 200,000. If this went on the French Army would be ruined. He therefore was of the opinion that 1 July was the latest date for the combined offensive of the British and the French.[2]

Haig would have preferred a mid-August launch of the Somme battle. He wanted as much time as possible to amass artillery and shells and complete the training of his troops. However, Joffre's insistence prevailed and so it was that when the British Army undertook its major offensive of 1916 – the Battle of the Somme – neither the place nor the time were of its commander's choosing. Moreover, as 1 July came nearer, the balance between the French and the British participation in the offensive changed dramatically. Because of the desperate need for reinforcements at Verdun the promised forty French divisions were steadily reduced. By June the number had fallen to nineteen and when the battle started on 1 July the French contribution was down to five. As a result, the French were to attack over a front of 8 miles with the British covering 16 miles. Instead of France being the major power in the joint offensive, the Somme had become a predominantly British battle.

The plan was simple. There would be a massive and unprecedented bombardment of the German lines lasting seven days and nights. This would pulverise the enemy trenches, destroy their barbed wire and kill off most of the defenders. Any surviving Germans would be in a state of extreme shock with their morale shattered. The raw British troops would then be able to walk across No-Man's-Land in extended line and occupy the undefended enemy lines. After the first German trenches had been occupied, the process would be repeated on successive enemy positions until the breakthrough was achieved.

What actually happened has been described as 'a catastrophe without parallel in British history'.[3] The artillery had in most places failed to destroy the German wire, and the German dugouts, built deep into the chalk, had survived the pounding of the British shells. When the barrage lifted from the German front line, their machine gun teams leapt out of their dugouts and started to fire on the slowly advancing British troops. The 'wave' formations were impossible to miss and the losses were appalling. By the end of the first day of the offensive the British had suffered 57,000 casualties of whom some 19,000 were dead. The Somme, far from providing a major breakthrough, became a long drawn-out battle of cruel attrition. The whole battle lasted 141 days and was eventually called off in late November. By that time the Allied losses had amounted to 615,000 (British 420,000 and French 195,000). German losses totalled 465,000.

* * *

Just as events at Verdun had determined the timing of the Somme offensive, so events on the Somme determined the timing of the attack at Fromelles. They also determined the fate of the British troops who happened to be in the Fromelles area and these included The Lee men of the 2/1st Bucks.

Despite the British disaster of 1 July, Haig remained optimistic: 'prospects were encouraging . . . and the next few days may very possibly place us in possession of the enemy's defences between the Ancre and the Somme'.[4] With this in mind, Haig, on 5 July, ordered the commanders of the British First and Second Armies, Gens Monro and Plumer, to 'select a front on which to pierce the enemy's lines'. The assumption was that British progress on the Somme would cause the Germans to transfer reinforcements from neighbouring sectors. This would leave the British First and Second Armies, positioned north of the Somme, facing an enemy that was 'much weakened and shaken and possibly contemplating retreat'.

Gen Plumer (Second Army) suggested to Gen Monro (First Army) that a joint operation should take place at the junction of their two armies and Monro agreed. The boundary between the First and Second Armies ran roughly on the west-to-east line Merville, Estaires, Laventie – some 40 miles north of the main Somme offensive. The First Army corps commander in that sector was Lt Gen Sir Richard Haking, and on 8 July Monro ordered him to put forward a scheme for an attack. Haking quickly came up with a plan to capture Aubers Ridge including the two villages of Aubers and Fromelles. It was ground well known to Haking – he had commanded a division there during the disastrous Aubers attack in May 1915. Monro, however, considered the proposal far too ambitious and vetoed it.

In any event, the nature of the intended attack was changing. Maj Gen Butler, Haig's Deputy Chief of Staff, visited Gen Monro on 13 July and informed him that the Germans had withdrawn troops – estimated at nine battalions – from the Lille area to reinforce their Somme front. Haig now wanted an action that would keep the Germans where they were and prevent further troop movements. The early optimism concerning progress on the Somme had proved ill-founded. Instead of opening a second front 'to pierce the enemy's lines', the proposed attack was now to be a holding operation. Indeed, some of Haig's general staff favoured an engagement involving only the artillery: 'it would be a useful diversion and help the southern operation'.[5]

Haking, however, continued to plan for what would essentially be an infantry attack – though one that would have significant artillery support. The final plan, as agreed with Gen Monro, was that the British 61st Division, on the extreme left of the First Army, and the 5th Australian Division, on the extreme right of the Second Army, would make an attack on 17 July. Both divisions would be under the command of Lt Gen Haking. The objective, as set out in the

A German observation post on Aubers Ridge.
(IWM E(AUS)4046)

First Army Order No. 100, was to 'capture and hold the German front line and support trenches from the Fauquissart–Trivolet Road to south of Cordonnerie Farm–Delangre Farm'.[6]

The junction of the Australian 5th Division and the British 61st Division was the Bond Street communication trench. From left to right (looking towards the German lines), the Australian 5th Division was made up of the 8th, 14th and 15th Brigades and the British 61st Division by the 184th, 183rd and 182nd Brigades. Each brigade was to use two of its four battalions in the attack, with the remaining two being held back in reserve. Similarly, each battalion would use only two of its four companies in the opening assault. The idea, therefore, was that around a quarter of the troops of the two divisions – about 5,000 men – would lead the assault with reserve troops available as reinforcements or to take over captured enemy positions. Facing the Australian and British positions was the 6th Bavarian Reserve Division made up of the 20th, 21st, 16th and 17th Bavarian Reserve Regiments – a total force of about 12,000 men.[7]

The British preliminary bombardment started on 14 July and this was supported by a diversionary bombardment 7 miles to the south, astride the La Bassée canal, in the hope that the Germans would transfer guns from the attack area. The purpose of the preliminary bombardment, as directed by Gen Monro, was to 'give the impression of an offensive operation on a large scale', but the real objective was to be limited to a 'purely local attack' on the enemy front line.[8] In other words, the emphasis of the attack had changed once more: at first an attack to open a second front; next an attack

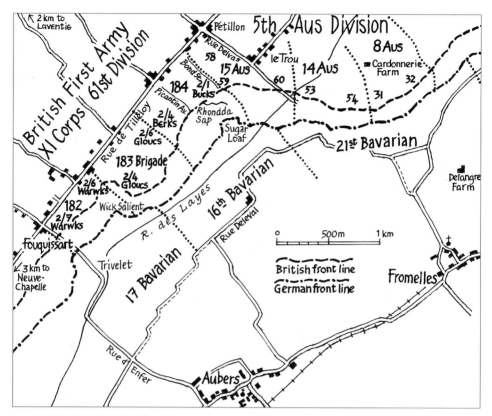

The battle order for the attack at Fromelles, 19/20 July 1916.

to prevent the transfer of troops; then a purely artillery operation; and now, finally, it was to be a feint, a bluff to divert the enemy's attention from the Somme. However, the latest change meant that there was now little need for secrecy – quite the opposite. The more the Germans believed that a major assault was imminent, the less likely they were to transfer their troops to the Somme. Indeed, they might even draw reinforcements into the Fromelles area from other parts of their line.

In fact, secrecy never was an option. The Germans could see everything that was going on as they looked towards Laventie from their positions on Aubers Ridge. Observers, high in the fortified tower of the church in Fromelles, had a clear view of the frenzied activity that was taking place in the British communication and front-line trenches. As Christie-Miller pointed out: 'The concentration of transport columns on all roads from Laventie to the front line was obvious.'

The Germans were therefore expecting an attack to take place – and they were well prepared to meet it. The regiments of the Bavarian 6th Reserve Division had held this same stretch of line since spring 1915 and they had developed a formidable defence system. The *British Official History* notes that: 'As little fighting had taken place in this region for the past fourteen months, the Germans had had

The view from the German observation post built inside the church tower at Fromelles looking across the attack area. *(IWM E(AUS) 4032)*

Soldiers of the 16th Bavarian Reserve Regiment near Fromelles, May 1916. (*Courtesy of Bayerisches Hauptstaatsarchiv*)

ample opportunity to strengthen their breastwork defences, which now included many machine gun emplacements constructed of concrete, well-sited and concealed.'9 The 16th Bavarian Reserve Regiment, for example, in the centre of the proposed attack area, had constructed seventy-five concrete emplacements along their 2,000-yard front. The strongest of these emplacements were sited on their main fortification, the Sugar Loaf salient. The Sugar Loaf protruded into No-Man's-Land and was so positioned that the fire from its machine guns covered the entire central section of the assault area. It was to become the key factor in the forthcoming attack.

* * *

The task of destroying the German wire and strongpoints in front of Fromelles rested squarely with the British and Australian artillery. It was clear that an effective artillery bombardment would pave the way for a successful infantry attack and it was equally clear that if the German machine gun emplacements remained largely intact then the infantry would face well-nigh impossible odds.

The artillery from the British 61st Division and the Australian 5th Division was, for the purposes of the attack, reinforced by batteries from other parts of the First and Second Armies. In total, 296 field guns and howitzers and 78 heavier pieces were deployed over the 4,200-yard front. The ammunition allotted to the attack was: 200,000 rounds for the field guns; 15,000 for the 4.5-in howitzers; and a total of 4,350 for the heavy and siege guns.[10] This was an impressive force and, proportionately, was even greater in density than the artillery used on the opening day of the Somme. On the morning of 14 July those batteries that were in position began their task of cutting the German barbed wire. The heavy artillery opened up on 16 July. Lt Gen Haking was full of confidence. At a conference on 16 July he told his divisional commanders that 'the narrow depth of the attack should make it possible, with the ammunition available, to reduce the defenders to a state of collapse before the assault.'[11]

Even at this late stage, twenty-four hours before the proposed attack, there took place yet another development in the preparations for Fromelles. On 16 July Maj Gen Butler paid a second visit to the First Army Headquarters at Chocques. He now informed Gens Monro and Plumer, with Lt Gen Haking present, that there was no urgent need for the XI Corps operation.

> Sir Douglas Haig did not wish the attack to take place at all unless it was considered that the artillery preparations had been adequate and unless the commanders concerned were satisfied, so far as it was humanly possible to foresee, that they had sufficient artillery and sufficient ammunition, not only to make the success of the attack assured, but to retain and consolidate the trenches gained.[12]

Why this apparent change of mind took place is not entirely clear. Haig, as a result of his recent experiences on the Somme, may have had second thoughts about using inexperienced troops in an attack that had diminished in strategic importance. Certainly, several officers in Haig's GHQ were having serious doubts about the likely success of the venture. Maj Howard, one of Haig's staff, had visited the Australian trenches in front of the Sugar Loaf and, in conversation with Brig Gen Elliott of the 15th Brigade, had given his opinion 'that the attack could hardly fail to end in disaster'.[13] Both Monro and Haking, however, remained confident of success and were against cancellation. The First Army Report on Fromelles records that 'the GOC XI Corps [Haking] pointed out that the troops had been worked up ready for the attack and were anxious to carry it out . . . any cancellation or change of plans would have a bad effect'.[14]

A two-storey German observation post, in 1918, built in concrete inside an old house on the Fromelles–Le Mesnil ridge.
(IWM E(AUS) 4040)

Characteristically, Haking took the opportunity to raise, yet again, the question of attacking the entire Aubers Ridge, but Butler quickly dismissed the idea saying that the Commander in Chief forbade it. It was, however, confirmed, 'at the urgent wish of the local Generals',[15] that the Fromelles attack should take place.

Several hours later, on the same day, Monro and Haking were given a second chance to abort the operation. Heavy rain had fallen soon after Gen Butler had left Chocques and he made a special return journey to discuss the effects that the bad weather might have on the attack. Gen Monro was absent, but Butler impressed on Monro's staff officer, Lt Col

Wilson, that the Army commander had full discretion to either cancel or postpone the attack 'for reasons of weather or for any other cause'.[16]

The poor weather on 15 and 16 July was certainly a cause for concern and the rain and drizzle hampered the efforts of the artillery to register accurately on the German lines. Zero had been fixed for 4.00 a.m. on 17 July, but at 11.00 p.m. on 16 July it was postponed for four hours. The rain continued into 17 July and Haking now informed Gen Monro that a further postponement of at least twenty-four hours was necessary.

Gen Monro, having received Butler's latest message via Lt Col Wilson, was now ready to cancel the entire operation – and it was within his authority to do so. His immediate reaction, however, was to contact Gen Haig's headquarters reporting the postponement and asking if he was authorised, in the event of further bad weather, to cancel the operation. The reply from Haig repeated the message previously communicated by Butler on his first visit to Chocques: 'The Commander in Chief wishes the special operation . . . to be carried out as soon as possible, weather permitting, provided always that Sir Charles Monro is satisfied that the conditions are favourable and that the reserves at his disposal, including ammunition, are adequate both for the preparation and execution of the enterprise.'[17]

Monro was therefore left to make the decision and since, only twenty-four hours earlier, he had expressed to Butler his confidence in the success of the operation, it was now almost impossible for him to change his opinion. Consequently, the order was issued from the First Army headquarters that the infantry attack would take place two days later on 19 July at 6.00 p.m.

* * *

The morning of 18 July was cloudy, but the sky cleared in the afternoon enabling the artillery to resume its bombardment of the German trenches. Dawn on 19 July was hazy and, since there were signs of more settled weather, Haking confirmed that a specially devised pre-attack artillery programme should begin at 11.00 a.m. and last seven hours. The last three hours of the artillery programme contained some novel features. The British 184th Infantry Brigade Order No. 16 (Appendix A) dated 16 July has a section headed 'Lifts'. During the period from 3.00 p.m. until 5.30 p.m. there would be four 'lifts' each lasting five minutes.

> During these 'lifts' the infantry in the trenches will show their bayonets over the parapet: dummy heads and shoulders will be shown over the parapet. Officers will whistle and shout orders in order to induce the enemy to man his parapet. At the end of each of these 'lifts' the Artillery will shorten range on to the enemy's front parapet and continue the intense bombardment of the front and support lines.[18]

Christie-Miller, observing these 'lifts' from the 2/1st Bucks Headquarters just behind the front line, described them as 'picturesque' and commented that the whole procedure 'gave a Biblical flavour to the proceedings, and the shouting and waving of bayonets took one back to the walls of Jericho'.[19]

But had the five-day artillery bombardment been effective? As might be expected, Haking had no doubts. In a letter read to all troops on 16 July he wrote: 'When we have cut all the wire, destroyed all the enemy's machine gun emplacements, knocked down most of his parapets, killed a large proportion of the enemy, and thoroughly frightened the remainder, our infantry will assault, capture, and hold the enemy's support line along the whole front.'[20] To the troops in the British front line the bombardment certainly appeared to be effective. Ivor Stewart-Liberty described the view from the 2/1st Bucks trenches: 'We had only to peer over the top to be filled with an unholy joy at the sight of the German trenches. Our 'stuff' was churning up the German lines into mere mounds of earth, and their losses must have been terrible.'[21] The accounts of the Bavarian regiments confirm that considerable destruction was caused and casualties inflicted. The history of the List Regiment (16th Bavarian Reserve), who were facing the 2/1st Bucks, records: 'Shortly after 5.00 p.m. all telephone communications ceased and the Battalion Commander sent out runners to find out what the situation was in the front line. They came back and reported that the dugout was under heavy and continuous fire, the losses were considerable and the positions were badly damaged.'[22] On 3 August, a German newspaper, the North German Gazette, made the following report on Fromelles: 'The trenches had suffered severely under the heavy bombardment and the wire entanglements had been completely swept away. The first line was completely wrecked and our losses were, naturally, not light.'[23]

However, despite the appearance of destruction and havoc in the German lines the true effect of the bombardment was extremely uneven. In some parts of the German line the wire and trench systems had been broken but in other parts they were intact. British infantry patrols, sent out during the night of 18 July, brought back mixed reports. The patrols from the 5th Australian Division reported that while there were several gaps in the German wire to the left of their front, the wire around the Sugar Loaf salient and in the centre of the attack line was intact. The conclusion reached in the *British Official History* is that the Fromelles bombardment gave only an illusion of success: 'The British bombardment appeared to be dealing faithfully with the German parapet, but it was not, in fact accomplishing the destruction essential to the success of the infantry assault.'[24] What the bombardment had failed to achieve was the destruction of the German dugouts and concrete emplacements.

There were several reasons for this general failure. Not all batteries had been in position for the opening bombardment on 14 July and, when in position, their efforts at accurate registration had been frustrated by poor weather conditions. This situation was not helped by the fact that a significant proportion of the artillery units lacked operational experience. The Australian artillery had no trained trench-mortar personnel and no experience on the Western Front. Some of their heavy batteries were newly formed and had never previously fired in France. The accuracy of certain batteries – both British and Australian – was extremely suspect: as witnessed by the front-line troops. Christie-Miller was emphatic: 'It should be said here that some of the artillery shooting was bad, notably that of an Australian battery.'[25] It was not unusual for artillery shells to fall short causing needless damage and casualties in the front trenches. Budgie Cummins had written some lines, with obvious feeling, a few days before his departure from the front-line trenches:

Now it's pleasant enough when one is feeling well
To hear artillery raising hell,
As long as they keep on each others O.P. [Observation Post]
And don't drop one short betwixt you and me.

The tactic of using 'lifts' during the last three hours of the British bombardment to lure the German troops to the parapets had no effect. The report in the *North German Gazette* was dismissive: 'it was only a ruse which the English are very fond of playing'.

The most critical failure of the bombardment was that it did not destroy the German strongpoints. Of the seventy-five concrete emplacements along the 16th Bavarian Reserve Regiment's front – which included the Sugar Loaf – only eight were destroyed and seven damaged, leaving sixty completely intact.[26] Moreover, the Germans had withdrawn most of their front-line troops to safer ground in the rear leaving only machine gun crews in their well-defended shelters. The British and Australian artillery may have

German pillboxes facing the Australian Brigade. These concrete emplacements were originally covered by sandbags and earthwork. *(IWM E(AUS) 3970)*

appeared to have caused severe damage to the German lines, but much of the shelling missed the machine gun emplacements or was expended on areas empty of German troops. Christie-Miller gave his assessment of the bombardment. It was damning: 'No effective destruction or neutralising of Hun Infantry, Artillery or Machine Guns took place. The total effect of our artillery preparations on the Hun resistance was nil.'[27]

The British bombardment had a further negative effect: it incited retaliation. The German artillery sited on Aubers Ridge with its commanding view of the British trench system was able to pinpoint the positions of the British infantry and artillery units. When the British guns opened up on 14 July the Germans were quick to respond. The British observation posts along the Rue Tilleloy, just behind the front line, were continually pounded, causing heavy casualties particularly among the gunner subalterns who were positioned there. Christie-Miller commented that during the final British bombardment on 19 July

> the enemy reply on our front line and communications and his counter-battery work were vigorous and effective during the whole day. Our front line was battered about and the casualties were heavy . . . 00 Battery R.H.A. were put in the open in full view of Aubers Ridge. Their services on the 19th were naturally of short duration.[28]

Private E. Penny, an Australian stretcher-bearer, noted in his pocket book that on 15 July the German bombardment caused 400 casualties.[29] Sapper Hollwey, of the 3/1st (South Midlands Field Company) Royal Engineers, wrote about the shelling on 19 July: 'Fairly quiet until 11.00 a.m. when our artillery started gradually working up until at 1.00 p.m. it was nothing but one huge roar. About 1.30 p.m. Fritz started to retaliate in earnest and then we had just hell until 5.30 p.m. every one of us expecting to get blowed to pieces.'[30]

* * *

The shelling of the key part of the German line – that directed against the Sugar Loaf salient – was causing particular concern to the British Command. The Sugar Loaf was heavily defended by concrete bunkers each housing machine gun crews, and its destruction was crucial to the success of the assault. Even on the afternoon of the 19 July there was evidence that the wire in front of the Sugar Loaf was undamaged. Reports to the First Army headquarters indicated that 'the bombardment was proceeding satisfactorily, except against the Sugar Loaf'. Instructions were accordingly issued for the heavy artillery to carry out an additional bombardment to begin at 2.35 p.m. This message, however, did not reach the British batteries opposite the Sugar Loaf until 5.10 p.m. A pencilled note across the message reads: 'Told R.A. [artillery]. Too late.'[31] This breakdown in communication was soon to have serious consequences.

The remains of the Sugar Loaf and its concrete shelters, seen in November 1918. *(IWM E(AUS) 3964)*

The troops who had the greatest interest in the circumstances around the Sugar Loaf were those of the 59th Australian and the 2/1st Bucks Battalions. The 2/1st Bucks were positioned in the centre of the line of attack with the 59th Australian Battalion on their left. The 2/1st Bucks were to attack on a 300-yard front, Bond Street–Picanton Avenue, and it was their task, along with the 59th Australian Battalion, to take the Sugar Loaf. At this point of the front line, just behind the German trenches, ran the River Laies – a drainage ditch about five feet wide and two feet deep. The Objective of the 2/1st Bucks, as set out in the 184th Brigade Instructions, issued on 16 July, was 'to capture and occupy the German front and support lines this side of the River Laies'.[32]

The few days before the attack had been particularly exhausting for the 2/1st Bucks. Christie-Miller records:

From the moment we arrived in the Laventie North area, the troops were practically engaged every night in the line or on working parties in preparation for the attack . . . We brought up hundreds of preserved rations and tins of water, thousands of Mills bombs, wire and picquets in profusion and an abundance of trench mortar ammunition – a respectable load for a couple of battalions for a couple of nights.

A particularly exhausting job was the removal of gas cylinders from the British front line. Some 1,500 cylinders, each weighing about 80lb and requiring four men to carry them – two handling and two resting – had been brought into the trenches in mid-June to be used in the course of normal trench warfare. Some gas had, in fact, been released in the Fauquissart area on 15 July. But now, because of the accuracy of the German artillery, these cylinders had become a dangerous hazard. Between 16 and 19 July every available soldier was employed to manhandle these cylinders away from the front. The *British Official History* states that 'some 470 cylinders were taken out, but the men were by then completely exhausted and no more cylinders could be moved'.[33]

The presence of gas cylinders proved particularly lethal in the trenches of the 2/1st Bucks. On 18 July an Australian battery

> dropped several H.E. shells in the front line and dropped one in A Company which, of course, burst and with enfilade wind spread the gas down the line instantly causing between 70/80 casualties including one officer, Lieut. Pitcher and some of the best N.C.O.s. In addition, Capt. Harold Church and his C.S.M., Arthur Brown, both of A Company, got a slight dose, but did not report sick.[34]

The Battalion suffered further severe casualties just before the attack. The German artillery was firing accurately on the 2/1st Bucks front line, now crowded with assault troops, and by 5.30 p.m., half an hour before zero, nearly a hundred men had been killed or wounded by shell-fire.

A Company [Capt H. Church] and D Company [Capt I.
Stewart-Liberty] had been designated as the assault
companies with B and C Companies remaining in reserve.
However, because of the casualties of the previous two days,
most of C Company was redeployed to make up the gaps
particularly in A Company. Apart from the HQ group and
transport the great majority of the Battalion had become
committed to the assault.

When the attack planned for 17 July was postponed, the
Bucks assault companies, A and D, were allowed to
withdraw to a rest area close to Laventie. Ivor Stewart-
Liberty wrote later:

We spent the night [of 18 July] two miles behind the
line in a ruined cottage; what was left of the building
afforded little or no shelter and most of us slept in the
open. Capt. Church, Sergt. Major A. Brown, Sergt.
Major R. Brown and myself slept within six yards of
each other. It was a fine night and everyone slept well.
At six the next morning we were at breakfast, a good
meal with, I remember, an extra ration of tobacco and
cigarettes. At seven we were off to the trenches, parties
of six in single file to avoid giving the German gunners
a good target. We arrived in the trenches (where I met
Lieut. P.C. Phipps[35] who had spent the night there)
without mishap. It was a beautiful morning and no
sound of war could be heard. The order of attack had to
be arranged, the way spied out, bombs to be prepared
and a thousand and one other things to be fixed up.

At the appointed hour [11.00 a.m.] our guns and trench-mortars started the bombardment; everyone took what shelter there was in the firing bays and it was not many minutes before the Germans 'opened-out'. Now started the worst part of modern battle. There we sat unable to do anything while the enemy battered our trenches and many a good man was wounded and killed. Sergt. Major R. Brown (you must remember I only know about the men who were close to me) and other brave spirits were busy all the time binding up the wounds of their comrades . . . So the day wore on with its incessant din and every minute seemed to see another good man knocked out. By the time the hour for the assault arrived we were all boiling with anger and only too eager to get to grips with 'Master Bosch' and to use the cold steel and bludgeon which many of us carried.[36]

Charles Phipps's pocket diary records the events of the days leading up to the attack:

16 July: Fatigues. Carrying stuff up to trenches. Get ready for the attack.
17 July: Attack postponed. Go back to billets 10.00 p.m. *Very* pleased to get back.
18 July: Relieve A Company who were gassed by our shell landing on one of our cylinders.

The entry in Charles Phipps's diary for 19 July simply reads: 'Zero hour fixed for today.' They were the last words he wrote.[37]

CHAPTER SIX

FROMELLES – THE ATTACK

A Minor Operation . . . To Assist Main Offensive (Somme).
Weekly Report on Operations – First Army 14–21 July 1916

Along the line of the Fromelles attack, the opposing trenches were between 100 and 400 yards apart. No-man's-land was flat, open and waterlogged and it was under heavy fire from German artillery and machine guns. It was across this hostile and forbidding ground that the British and Australian troops were now committed to advance towards the strongly held German positions.

At 5.40 p.m. (20 minutes before zero hour) on Wednesday 19 July, the assault companies of the 2/1st Bucks moved into No-Man's-Land through sally ports: gaps that had been made in their sandbagged parapets the previous night. The German machine guns had opened up 10 minutes earlier – confirming the widely held suspicion that the enemy were well aware of the British plans. There were rumours that the Germans had found the details of the assault on the body of a British officer just hours before the attack took place. It is also possible that the Germans were able to intercept British telephone messages and, several days after the attack, German listening apparatus was found in one of the 183rd

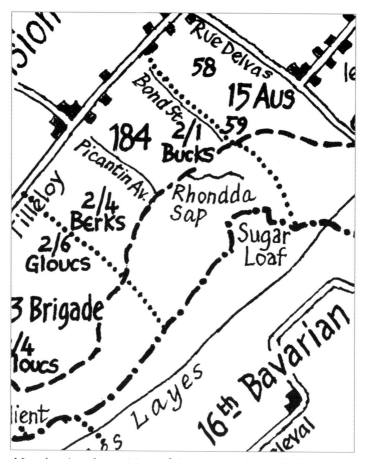

Map showing the positions of the 2/1st Bucks, 2/4th Berks, and 58th and 59th Australian Battalions opposite the Sugar Loaf.

Brigade trenches. However, it is equally possible that the Germans had simply inferred the time of the attack from the pattern of the British barrage. In any event, the Bavarian machine gun crews were clearly ready and waiting for the assault well before zero hour.

The use of sally ports, stipulated in the divisional orders, turned out to be a major error. The German machine gun

The remains of a German bunker on the German front line opposite 14th Australian Brigade.

positions on the Sugar Loaf had clearly not been destroyed by the British artillery and the sally ports were ideal targets. Movement through them soon became impossible. They were death traps. Ivor Stewart-Liberty wrote: 'Those infernal machine guns had started their rattle, and all must have realised that the chances of their return were small indeed'.[1]

The records of the 16th Bavarian Reserve Regiment describe the scene at the start of the attack:

The English jumped over their breastworks and began to attack our position. While they tried to unravel themselves [from the sally ports] they were met head on by the fire of our infantry machine guns. This caused disorder and confusion throughout their ranks . . . Again and again the English tried in vain to form firing lines and press forward. The fire of the German infantry and the bursts from the machine guns decimated their ranks. Heroic English officers with drawn bayonets rushed forward to encourage their men by example. They were mown down . . .[2]

Realising the chaos caused by the sally ports, Lt Col Williams, the CO of the 2/1st Bucks, ordered their use to be abandoned. Instead, he directed the assault troops into No-Man's-Land by way of Rhondda Sap: a short trench that had been dug some 70 yards towards the enemy lines. By zero hour, the depleted A and D Companies, reinforced by part of C Company, were in position and at 6.00 p.m. exactly they made their attack. Christie-Miller wrote about the advance: 'It has been described as magnificent. Not a man was seen to waver.' Stewart-Liberty later said:

I have never been so proud in my life as when the moment came; every man was eager, nay more than eager, to be there first . . . Everyone seemed excited and mad to be in the German trenches to avenge their friends who had already fallen. No-one thought of himself or of his own danger. It was splendid . . . I never saw one man flinch.[3]

But there was no avoiding the tragic events that followed. The Battalion Diary of the 2/1st Bucks records: 'With a cheer the two waves leapt up and assaulted the enemy trenches . . . the enemy's machine guns had become busy and at 6.00 p.m. they mowed down our advancing waves so that only a few men actually reached the German parapet. These men did not return.'[4] Spr W.H. Hollwey of the 3/1st (South Midlands) Field Company, who observed the assault, noted in his diary: 'It was suicide to try and get across.'[5]

It was all too clear that the enemy strongpoints on the Sugar Loaf were largely undamaged. The 2/1st Bucks, coming out of Rhondda Sap, had to cover a further 250 yards of open ground to reach the Sugar Loaf. It proved impossible. According to Christie-Miller: 'The fire brought to bear was annihilating. Hardly a man, if any, reached the German parapet – though it was said that L/Cpl Stevens of D Company was seen to reach it.' Stewart-Liberty remembered that

> The German machine guns, until now hidden deep in the ground, swept among us . . . Some got to the German trenches; some got only a few yards . . . I saw one wounded man binding up his 'pal'. He had hardly started when he got another bullet through his back which killed him. Private Arnold Morris I lost sight of, although we went out together. Sergt Major Ralph Brown was hit. Private Sydney Dwight I did not see after I left the trenches. The other Lee men who fell were with Capt. Church.[6]

The British and Australian *Histories* confirm these accounts. The Sugar Loaf defences remained intact and the machine guns sited there destroyed the Bucks attack:

Arnold Morris with his wife Emily and two children, 1915.

The two [Bucks] Companies that deployed via Rhondda Sap did so in a hail of shrapnel. The right Company [D] was practically destroyed in its efforts to advance, but on the left a party [A Coy] reached the north-east face of the salient. There was sharp fighting on the parapet until all were killed or wounded. A third company [C], bearing material for consolidation, left the line at 6.10 pm, but was stopped by the fire of German machine guns.[7]

On the left, Capt. Church, leading his Company [A], was killed as he reached the German breastwork, and, according to some accounts, a small section of the western face of the Sugar Loaf was entered.[8]

Capt Harold Church reached the Sugar Loaf before being killed.

Even before 6.30 p.m. it was clear that the Bucks attack had failed: 'Three hundred men went out and one hundred men got back.'9 All the officers of the combined A and C Companies were killed and all those of D Company were wounded. Of The Lee men, Charles Phipps had his leg shattered early in the attack. He was being carried back to the trenches by his batman, Pte Sydney Damant, when they were both caught by machine gun fire. Charles Phipps was killed immediately and Sydney Damant died from his wounds six days later. Arthur Brown, Edward Sharp, Sydney Dwight, Arnold Morris and Percy Price all just disappeared

– their bodies were never found. Harry Harding was wounded, taken prisoner and died shortly after his capture. Ralph Brown was fatally wounded, shot in the stomach, and died the following day.

Ivor Stewart-Liberty, leading his company towards the enemy lines, was severely wounded in the left leg. Pte Cook, Ralph Brown's batman, immediately stopped to help, but was ordered by Stewart-Liberty to press on with the attack. Pte Cook was never seen again. Shortly afterwards, Sgt Charles Austin also offered assistance. Ivor Stewart-Liberty later wrote:

I had been hit. Sergt. Austin, who had already been wounded, crawled to me and, on his knees, began to bind my wounds. No sooner had he started than he was hit again in the back. He lay close to me for some time and eventually managed to get into a shell hole. He was later captured and died a prisoner of war. I should like it to be known that this brave man died through tending me.[10]

Ivor Stewart-Liberty lay helpless in No-Man's-Land until it became dark and was eventually rescued by one of his sergeants, Joseph Petty. Petty dragged Stewart-Liberty – at one time mistakenly towards the German lines – for five hours before regaining the Bucks trenches.

Of The Lee men who took part in the assault only Arthur Rutland emerged from the Fromelles attack unscathed. He was to die from nephritis in Rouen in March 1917.

The poet Ivor Gurney served at Fromelles as a private in the 2/5th Glosters. Some years later he wrote:

Who died on the wires, and hung there, one of two –
Who for his hours of life had chattered through
Infinitely lovely chatter of Bucks accent:
Yet faced unbroken wires; stepped over and went
A noble fool, faithful to his stripes – and ended.[11]

* * *

The other battalions along the 61st Division front had mixed fortunes. On the extreme right, towards the Fauquissart–Trivolet line (182nd Brigade), the 2/7th Warwicks deployed into No-Man's-Land with hardly any loss and rushed the German front line from fifty yards. They found the wire and breastworks completely destroyed and for a time took possession of both the front and reserve German lines. But soon the Germans counter-attacked and the 2/7th Warwicks were caught in crossfire losing many men and causing them to fall back from the enemy trenches. Next to them, the 2/6th Warwicks lost heavily as they advanced into No-Man's-Land and were finally checked in front of the German wire – completely intact – on Wick salient. The Australian *History* describes how the soldiers of the 17th Bavarian Reserve Regiment emerged from their dugouts behind their front line and raced the 2/6th Warwicks to the breastworks. The Warwicks were only fifty yards from the Bavarians when the enemy machine guns opened fire. In a matter of seconds the Warwicks lost 9 officers and 220 men. The few men who pressed on were shot down before they reached the enemy parapet.

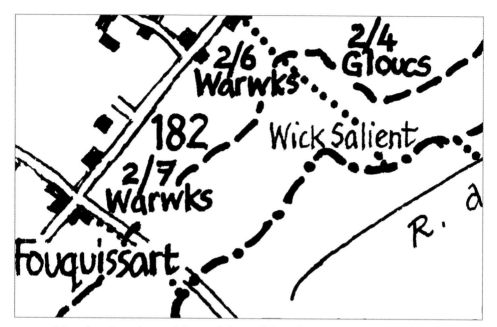

Map showing the positions of the 2/6th and 2/7th Warwicks opposite the Wick Salient.

The 183rd Brigade attacked from their lines in front of the hamlet of Le Tilleloy. The two assault battalions, the 2/4th and the 2/6th Glosters, had been heavily shelled while still in their trenches, the 2/6th losing fifty men. Both battalions suffered heavy casualties from shrapnel as they deployed through the sally ports. Once in No-Man's-Land the Gloster battalions were strafed by machine gun fire and those few who succeeded in reaching the German wire were soon killed or wounded.

On the left of the divisional front (184th Brigade), the assaulting troops, alongside the 2/1st Bucks, were the 2/4th Berks. The Berks also suffered badly as they went through

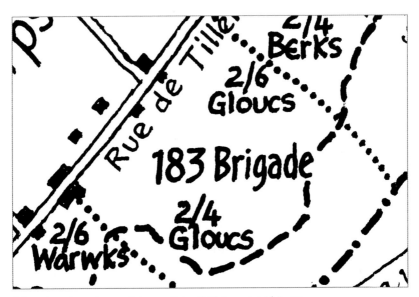

Map showing the positions of the 2/6th and 2/4th Glosters.

the sally ports. Two platoons managed to reach the enemy wire, which they found uncut, but they were forced back through lack of support on their flanks.

By 6.30 p.m., only half an hour after the start of the attack, the situation on the British 61st Division front was extremely serious. Some temporary progress had been made on the extreme right, but generally the attack had been thrown back with heavy casualties and the Germans were still in possession of their trenches. In particular, they still held the Sugar Loaf and this was to have a critical effect on the efforts of the Australian 5th Division. Fromelles was to prove a greater disaster for the Australians than it was for the British.

* * *

About half of the Australian troops had already seen active service in Gallipoli, but they were new to the Western Front. Fromelles was their first battle in France. In fact, of the six Australian assault battalions, three had not seen the front-line trenches until they reached their assault positions only a few hours before zero and the other three had been in the front line no longer than two days. Nevertheless, as the Australian *History* points out:

> The 14th and 15th Brigades contained about 25 per cent of well-seasoned men [from Gallipoli] and the majority of their officers and N.C.O.s had fought at ANZAC.[12] The 8th, on the other hand, though long and carefully trained, were entirely new to fighting. [The assault battalions], however, were composed of older and hardened men – miners, farmers and bush workers from Southern Australia and Queensland.

Despite their lack of experience on the Western Front the Australians were a formidable force and they were determined to prove their worth.

On the far left of the attack, the Australians exploded a mine containing 1200 lb of ammonal in No-Man's-Land at zero hour. The purpose was to create a barrier – the debris from the explosion – that would protect the flanks of the 31st and 32nd Battalions (8th Brigade) from enemy enfilade fire. The Germans, however, were still able to man their machine guns and fire into the advancing Australian troops. It was only with great determination, and not without

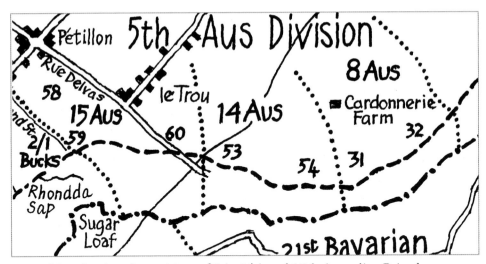

Map showing the positions of 8th, 14th and 15th Australian Brigades.

considerable losses, that the 31st and 32nd Battalions were able to press forward, take the German trenches and move to a point near Delangre Farm. By a curious coincidence, a local Buckinghamshire man was serving with the Australian 32nd Battalion. He was Pte Sydney James Lacey who had emigrated from Chesham four years previously. Pte Lacey had been in France only six weeks and he was among the dead of the 32nd on 19 July.

In the Australian centre, the 54th and 53rd Battalions of the 14th Brigade also managed to storm the enemy lines and advance some way past the German front line. But the troops of both the 8th and the 14th Brigades, once past the German front line, had been unable to find their ultimate objective: the enemy second-line positions. The trench maps provided by British Intelligence were inaccurate and it became clear that the enemy's support trench system, drawn neatly on the maps, just did not exist. Those German soldiers not in the heavily fortified front line were well to the rear in relative safety. The Australians therefore emerged into an area of flat, waterlogged ground intersected by ditches. Here isolated groups of men dug in and did what they could to consolidate their position by linking ditches and mud-filled shell holes.

On the left and in the centre the Australians had therefore largely achieved their objective. On the right, however, where the Australian 15th Brigade met the British 184th Brigade opposite the Sugar Loaf salient, the situation was quite different. Attacking next to the 2/1st Bucks, the Australian 59th Battalion crossed the River Laies, at this point in front of the German lines, and immediately came under machine gun fire from the Sugar Loaf. Their advance

The River Laies which ran across No-Man's-Land between the Australian 15th Brigade and the Sugar Loaf. *(IWM E(AUS) 3965)*

was checked with terrible losses and the survivors, stranded in No-Man's-Land, were unable to make further progress. On their left, the 60th Battalion managed to get to the German wire, but could move no further.

* * *

Maj Gen Mackenzie, the Commander of the British 61st Division, was, understandably in the confusion of the battle, receiving mixed accounts of the overall situation. But the picture as he understood it, around 7.30 p.m., gave him some cause for optimism: while there had been little progress in the centre of the division, the advance on the right flank had been successful. And he had even received a report that a foothold had been gained on the Sugar Loaf. Mackenzie, acting within his authority, therefore ordered all three British brigades to prepare for a further attack at 9.00 p.m.

Brig Carter, the commander of the British 184th Brigade, had a somewhat clearer idea of the dire situation in front of the Sugar Loaf. He was well aware that if the 2/1st Bucks were to renew their attack they would require considerable support from the Australians on their left flank. Consequently, when Carter received Mackenzie's order for the 9.00 p.m. attack, he immediately sent the following message, through the normal divisional channels, to the 15th Australian Brigade: 'Am attacking at 9.00 p.m. Can your right battalion co-operate?' Brig Elliott, commanding the 15th Australians, knew that the remains of his right battalion, the 59th, were in No-Man's-Land, unable to move.

Nevertheless, he took the courageous decision to bring up a fresh battalion, the 58th, for the 9.00 p.m. assault.[13]

Meanwhile, the true extent of the British 61st Division losses was gradually emerging. Most of the assault battalions had lost half of their troops. An attack at 9.00 p.m. was out of the question. Yet Christie-Miller of the 2/1st Bucks 'found it next to impossible to persuade the authorities that there was nothing left to attack with – the Battalion or what was left of it being mostly in No-Man's-Land and our trenches under intense bombardment'. Most of the survivors of the 2/7th Warwicks, who had captured the German trenches on the extreme right, had now fallen back to their own lines and the other battalions of the 61st Division were in no fit state to renew the offensive. Two of them (the 2/6th Glosters and the 2/4th Berks) had lost their commanding officers.

When Lt Gen Haking became aware of the overall situation he countermanded Mackenzie's order for the 9.00 p.m. attack. Consequently, at 8.30 p.m., Mackenzie sent a second message to the 5th Australian Division Headquarters: 'Under instructions from the Corps Commander am withdrawing from captured enemy line after dark.' However, owing, as the Australian *History* puts it, 'to a failure of the Headquarters of the [Australian] 5th Division', this message did not reach Gen Elliott of the 15th Australian Brigade until 9.25 p.m. By then it was all too late. The Australian 58th Battalion, together with the remains of the 59th already in No-Man's-Land, had already carried out the 9.00 p.m. attack on the Sugar Loaf entirely unsupported on either flank. The Australian *History* describes it as 'one of the bravest and most hopeless assaults ever undertaken by the Australian Imperial Force'.[14] Two-thirds of the way across No-Man's-Land the German machine guns on the Sugar Loaf opened up: 'The line was shattered and the men dazed . . . the two Companies of the 58th that had made the attack were practically annihilated'. The Sugar Loaf undisputedly remained in German hands.

On the left of the Australian line, the situation of the 14th and 8th Brigades had become increasingly untenable as they were bombed and counter-attacked by German reinforcements. By 3.15 a.m. on 20 July most of the Australians had been forced back to their trenches. In the meantime, Gen Monro, following a meeting with Lt Gen Haking and the two divisional commanders, had called for the withdrawal of all the troops still in No-Man's-Land and, at 5.00 a.m., the attack at Fromelles was abandoned. Just after 8.00 a.m., the Bavarian troops were able to 'join hands' (*die Hand zu reichen*) along their original front line.[15]

The British and German trench positions at Fromelles were therefore exactly the same as they had been fourteen hours earlier. During that time, the Australian 5th Division had lost 5,500 men and the British 61st Division 1,550. German casualties amounted to less than 2,000.

* * *

As a result of the attack at Fromelles, the 2/1st Bucks lost half their men.[16] On 17 July the Battalion numbered 20 officers and 642 other ranks. On 20 July there were 5 officers and 335 other ranks. The casualty figures were:

	Officers	*Other ranks*	*Total*
Killed	7	127	134
Wounded	8	180	188
Total	15	307	322

All the officers of A, C and D Companies were either killed or wounded and two officers – Maj Barrett and Capt Buckmaster – suffered breakdowns and were invalided back to England.

At 1.00 a.m. on 20 July, the remnants of the Battalion were relieved by the 2/4th Ox and Bucks and withdrew to billets north of Laventie. Later in the day they were transported to Estaires. Christie-Miller wrote:

> The first parade held in Estaires, when the Companies paraded as they had come out of the line, was one of the saddest I have ever attended . . . B Coy was fair sized, C Coy had two fair platoons and the rest of the Battalion was represented by a handful of men and practically without N.C.O.s. Of the Officers practically all those with experience had gone.[17]

While the Battalion was in Estaires it received a visit from the divisional commander, Maj Gen Mackenzie. Christie-Miller was unimpressed: 'The Divisional Commander addressed the battalion in a hesitating speech in which I for one could see no point, unless it was that in the next action perhaps we should do better.' After three days in Estaires, the Battalion moved to a camp west of Laventie and the process of reorganising and refitting began.

* * *

In the days following the attack every effort was made to bring in the wounded from No-Man's-Land. The 2/4th Ox and Bucks, now occupying the trenches previously held by the 2/1st Bucks, set about the task of finding and retrieving the wounded lying in front of the Sugar Loaf. There was spasmodic firing from the German lines making the work extremely hazardous. In bringing in the wounded the Ox and Bucks themselves lost fifty-eight men.

Pte E.C. Penny, a stretcher-bearer with the 58th Australian Battalion, also working in the Sugar Loaf area, recorded in his notebook:

> I was carrying wounded all night and most of next day [19–20 July] . . . the dead were lying in heaps, blown to pieces . . . [on 21 July] the firing line was quiet as both sides were still carrying out wounded and repairing trenches. Stretcher-bearers brought in many wounded from No-man's land. No armistice but a mutual understanding on both sides.

On occasions the 'mutual understanding' broke down: 'One German brought a wounded Australian over to our parapet, but was shot by one of 8th Brigade. As a consequence they shot one of our bearers and killed him and a man on a stretcher.'[18] Col J.C. Stewart of the 57th Australian Battalion noted: 'During the night (20th) the 57th brought in 200 wounded and 170 on night 21/22 July. As far as we know, the Germans did nothing.'[19]

The medical officer of the Australian 57th Battalion, Capt H. Rayson, later wrote: 'During the next week wounded continued to come down as a result of the 19th. These men had been rescued from No-man's land. As far as I can remember the last man reached my Post 9 or 10 days after the battle.'[20] According to the Australian medical records their main dressing stations dealt with 3,277 wounded.

On 20 July, just before noon, an event took place that has been the subject of controversy ever since. Pte Miles of the Australian 29th Battalion was searching in No-Man's-Land for a wounded comrade when he was confronted by a German officer. After some formalities, the German proposed to Miles that he should go back to his lines and return with an officer to discuss a possible ceasefire so that the wounded might be brought in. A Maj Murdoch agreed to go out with Miles. In the meantime, the German officer had received authority for a brief truce – the Australians would clear the wounded from their half of No-Man's-Land and the Germans would do likewise. During the period of the truce Murdoch was to remain in German hands as a hostage. Murdoch took this proposal back to his superiors and, after some delay, was told that the Australian divisional commander, Gen James McCay, had forbidden the truce to take place. Years later, McCay claimed that the British generals, Haking and Monro, had both subsequently approved his decision. Nevertheless, the opportunity to save many hundreds of lives – Australian, British and German – was lost. It was a decision that earned for McCay the hatred of many Australians and the title of 'The Butcher'.

* * *

Apart from the wounded, No-Man's-Land was thick with the dead. CSM Lockwood of the 2/5th Glosters made the following entry in his diary:

the ground was littered with dead . . . The cleaning-up after 19th July was petty grim. The number of men in No-man's Land was very great and July was a very hot month in France in 1916 and after a few days the stench was awful. We could not possibly get all the dead in. We had tried, but a stiff corpse is the most awkward thing to handle especially when he had died in some grotesque position. In any case, only one body could be brought in at a time on a stretcher and of course all our barbed wire had to be negotiated, which in the dark and harassed all the time by German fire, made things very difficult. I sweated on that job for several nights. It was a hopeless task and after about a week the idea was given up. Then somebody had the idea of burning the dead. I suppose the idea had points, but whoever had thought it had forgotten that the dead were not in convenient piles but were scattered from our wire to somewhere half way over in No-man's land. To do any good they had to be dragged together and made into a pile of some sort. I think I liked that job even less than the other one. We took tins of petrol with us and we made one pile to start the cremation. When the first blaze of petrol went up, well, of course the German sentries got curious and sprayed the whole area with gun-fire, and that was most unpleasant. So, in the end, that was abandoned. Sacks of chloride lime were finally brought into the line and the whole area was doused as much as it was possible to do with that. It did lessen the stench, but that part of the line always remained pretty grim.[21]

In the middle of this gruesome cleaning-up process there arrived the usual messages from the generals. Sir Douglas Haig, the British Commander in Chief, wrote (21 July): 'Please convey to the Troops engaged night 19/20 my appreciation for their most gallant effort and thorough preparation made for it. I wish them to realise that their enterprise has not been by any means in vain and that the gallantry with which they carried out the attack is fully recognised.'[22] Lt Gen Haking (20 July) sent the following message:

I wish to convey to all Ranks of your Division my appreciation of the gallant attack carried out yesterday by them. Although they were unable to consolidate the ground gained, the effect on the enemy will be far-reaching and will prevent them from moving Troops away from our front to the South. I wish you all in your next attack a more complete and permanent victory and that you may reap the full fruit of the energy and skill displayed by all commands and staff in the execution of their task.[23]

Maj Gen Mackenzie (20 July) wrote: 'The Division not only fought gallantly, but all ranks of every arm and service have carried out in the most exemplary and devoted manner working day and night, an amount of labour which has highly tested their endurance and discipline and merits my unqualified praise.'[24] Brig Gen Carter (20 July) addressed his comments directly at the 2/1st Bucks: 'Depleted as their ranks were, by gas on the evening previous, and also subjected to several enemy bombardments prior to the Assault of the 19 inst. (resulting in 100 casualties) the 2/1st Bucks in carrying out their attack proved beyond doubt that they are imbued with that grit and determination so essential to success in war . . . '.[25]

These expressions of appreciation, if somewhat banal, were no doubt well meaning and Brig Gen Carter's message was at least specific in its content. Lt Gen Haking's communication was, however, somewhat at odds with his comments made in the XI Corps Report to the First Army (24 July):

> The Australian Infantry attacked in the most gallant manner and gained the enemy's position, but they were not sufficiently trained to consolidate the ground gained . . . The [British] 61st Division were not sufficiently imbued with the offensive spirit to go in like one man at the appointed time . . . With two trained Divisions the position would have been a gift.

In an attached memo, Haking wrote: 'I think the attack, although it failed, has done both Divisions a great deal of good.'[26]

So, according to Lt Gen Haking, one division was 'not sufficiently trained' and the other lacked the 'offensive spirit'. These words can only be regarded as fatuous from a general who, along with his superior, Gen Monro, had argued strongly that the attack should take place and who had confirmed to the Commander in Chief that 'the reserves were adequate both for the preparation and the execution of the enterprise'. And anyone reading Haking's comment that the attack had done both divisions 'a great deal of good' must wonder how a 50 per cent casualty rate could have achieved that end.

More pertinent were the comments made in the 2/1st Bucks Battalion diary by their CO, Lt Col Williams:

One of the most striking lessons to be learnt from the attack is that the greatly superior method of holding trenches adopted by the Germans should at once be adopted by the British and French Armies . . . Whereas on our Battalion front the Regiment had not one bomb-proof shelter and lost 100 casualties from the shelling alone, the Germans appeared to have some 6 teams of machine guns and very few infantry. Even after seven hours bombardment by our guns these 6 teams of machine gunners appeared intact, firing over the parapet at our assaulting infantry. By crowding three Companies into three hundred yards of front our casualties from shell-fire were the more heavy.[27]

* * *

Any examination of Fromelles can only conclude that it was a disaster. From beginning to end, it was a catalogue of confused planning, indecision and tactical error. The strategic purpose of the attack was altered several times; the attack was declared unnecessary and yet allowed to continue; the inexperienced artillery failed to destroy the German strongpoints; secrecy and surprise were disregarded; the troops were exhausted through heavy labouring duties; and many casualties were caused because of the instruction to use sally ports. To these manmade errors were added the effects of ill fortune: the deterioration in the weather that hindered artillery preparations and, most poignantly, the failure of critical communications to arrive on time.

It is little wonder, therefore, that none of the objectives of the Fromelles attack was realised. The local objective – to take the first two German lines – was not remotely achieved and the Germans retained their positions around Fromelles until 1918. Even if the attack had been successful, the outcome would have been disastrous in that it would have brought the British front line under still closer enemy observation from Aubers Ridge making it an easy target for the German guns.

Fromelles also failed in its main strategic objective – to prevent the Germans from transferring troops south to the main battle on the Somme. The Germans saw Fromelles for what it was – a purely local attack of no major significance. It was a crude attempt at bluff and it fooled nobody. And, if the German High Command had any doubts about this, they were soon removed when documents found on the body of a

Fromelles 1919 – a scene of destruction. *(IWM E(AUS) 3963)*

British officer confirmed the limited purpose of the attack. Within days, the Germans had transferred their 183rd Division from the Somme to their Sixth Army in the north, and the Guard Reserve Corps was sent from the Fromelles area to Cambrai near the Somme. The Fromelles operation had no effect on the transfer of German troops – one way or the other.[28] Christie-Miller summarised the situation in his usual direct way: 'If the object was to keep the [German] troops in the North and impress them that we were going to make a serious effort on the Lys, it showed contempt for the Hun Intelligence Department which was never justified.'[29]

Both the British and the Australian *Official Histories* are highly critical of the attack. The verdict of the British *History* is that: 'The pity of it was that the action need not have been fought, since the First Army had perfect liberty to cancel it. To have delivered battle at all betrayed a great under-estimate of the enemy's power of resistance.'[30] The Australian *History* concludes: 'The reasons for the failure seem to have been loose thinking and somewhat reckless decision on the part of the higher staff . . . it is difficult to conceive that the operation, as planned, was ever likely to succeed.'[31]

In 1937, when the *British Official History* was being compiled, a number of officers who had served at Fromelles were invited to comment on the draft chapter covering that attack. Capt Wilfred Greene of the 2/1st Bucks, attached at the time to the 61st Division HQ, wrote:

> The operation was bound to be a costly failure. Those responsible for planning it showed a complete ignorance of the ground . . . no amount of preparation or training would have enabled a success to be made of an attack which was (a) tactically misconceived and (b) made with inadequate forces, inadequately supported by artillery over ground where it was not possible to consolidate the position if captured, dominated as it was.[32]

And Lt Col M.M. Parry-Jones, of the British 183rd Brigade, summarised his comments on the Fromelles draft chapter: 'What could be expected of such an attack but failure?'[33]

Brig Gen H.E. Elliott, the commander of the Australian 15th Brigade that had lost so many of its men in front of the Sugar Loaf, was particularly scathing in his comments on Fromelles:

The whole operation was so incredibly blundered from beginning to end that it is almost incomprehensible how the British Staff, who were responsible for it, could have consisted of trained professional soldiers of considerable reputation and experience, and why, in view of the outcome of this extraordinary adventure, any of them were retained in active command.[34]

In fact, a number of high-ranking officers were to lose their commands as a result of Fromelles. Fromelles was a failure and it had, in Christie-Miller's words, 'its proper complement of victims'. Among them were Gen Monro, the First Army commander, Brig Carter of the 184th Brigade and Brig Stewart of the 183rd Brigade. All three 'relinquished' their commands in late July 1916. Generally regarded as undeserving 'victims' were Lt Col Ames of the 2/4th Ox and Bucks and Lt Col Williams of the 2/1st Bucks who were sent back to England in August.

The removal of Lt Col Williams, who had been with the 2/1st Bucks since its formation in 1914, was regarded as particularly unjust. The entry in the 2/1st War Diary for 1 August 1916 reads: '1.00am. Lt. Col. Williams left by motor-car for Boulogne and England. His loss is deeply felt by the whole Battalion.' Christie-Miller, his second in command, wrote of Williams:

I say without hesitation, after close personal contact for almost 2 years, that he was by far the best C.O. of the Division . . . When the Battalion came to France, nothing could have exceeded his consideration for and his confidence in, his officers and it is true to say that at no time did he stand better with all the ranks of the Battn. than the day he was sent home with the victims.

Christie-Miller, in his comments about the 'victims' also pointedly remarked: 'The complement [of victims] was not in any way reduced by the fact that all orders complete in all detail came from Corps and no opportunity was given to any subordinate commander to initiate any operation of his own.'[35] The reference to 'Corps' was a direct comment on Lt Gen Haking who retained his position as commander of XI Corps until the end of the war.

A further regrettable outcome of Fromelles was that it gave rise to some considerable ill feeling among Australian troops towards the British. Such ill feeling had some justification in relation to the planning and general preparation of the assault, but the Australians extended their resentment to the actions of the British rank and file. The *Australian Official History* notes:

A particularly unfortunate, but almost inevitable result of the fight was that, having been unwisely combined with a British Division whose value for offence, in spite of the devoted gallantry of many of its members, was recognised as doubtful, the Australian soldiers tended to accept the judgement – often unjust, but already deeply impressed by the occurrences of the Suvla landing [in Gallipoli] – that the 'Tommies' could not be relied upon to uphold a flank in a stiff fight.

However, in a footnote, the Australian *History* at least concedes: 'The fate of Captain Church (2/1st Bucks), and several other officers, whose bodies, with those of their parties, were long afterwards found lying near the German wire, proves the quality of parts of this division.'[36] Fourteen years after the disaster at Fromelles, Brig Gen Elliott of the Australian 15th Brigade said of the British troops: 'We cannot justly blame their failure in the circumstances. Like ourselves, they were the victims of shocking generalship.'[37] In their comments on the draft chapter on Fromelles in the *British Official History*, Elliott's opinion was endorsed by several British officers. Hereward Wake of the 2/1st Bucks, wrote: 'The whole plan for the infantry depended on the effectiveness of the artillery plan. It was not fair to blame the troops for the failure.'[38] Referring to Gen Haking's criticism of the 61st Division, Wilfred Greene commented: 'I cannot help hoping that the Official History may find it possible to repudiate so gross a slander on a gallant Division which was massacred through no fault of its own.'[39]

* * *

In spite of everything, Fromelles was not without its heroes. Lt Gen Haking's comments on the shortcomings of the British and Australian rank and file were unworthy of the great effort and sacrifice made by the soldiers of these two divisions. Eyewitness accounts testify to the courage and bravery displayed by the troops both before and during the attempt to take the German lines. The number of medals awarded as a result of Fromelles is, of course, only an indicator of the outstanding courage of the men who fought there, particularly since it was the custom to give medals only to the survivors. It is worth recording, however, that an estimate[40] of the number of awards made to the Australian troops totals 217, made up of:

Distinguished Service Order	9
Military Cross	48
Distinguished Conduct Medal	45
Military Medal	63
Foreign Decorations	14
Mentioned in Despatches	38

There is no such overall breakdown of British awards because of incomplete records, though battalion diaries and histories give some indication. The records of the 2/1st Bucks are complete and they contain a list of awards for bravery made to members of that Battalion:

Military Cross	4
Distinguished Conduct Medal	2
Military Medal	9

Among those who were awarded the Military Cross was Ivor Stewart-Liberty. The citation reads: 'He displayed complete disregard of personal danger and by his fine example under heavy fire gave great encouragement to his men. He kept them together in the assault under heavy

Capt Ivor Stewart-Liberty MC, who lost a leg at Fromelles.

machine gun fire and led them to the enemy's trenches. He was severely wounded.' Sgt Joseph Petty, who rescued Ivor Stewart-Liberty, was awarded the Military Medal for saving his officer's life.[41] Stewart-Liberty later wrote that both Arthur Brown and Ralph Brown were to have been recommended for 'special distinction' for their 'splendid work and great bravery' both before and during the attack.[42] The two Brown brothers were, however, not among the survivors and consequently these recommendations were never processed.

CHAPTER SEVEN

THE LEGACY

The war will pass and there will be a future after it.
W.J. Beeson, *The Lee Magazine*, December 1915

A headline in the *Bucks Examiner* of 28 July 1916 read: 'A Heavy List of Local Casualties'. The report, which gave the names of local men who had recently been killed or wounded, continued:

> Friday last, 21st July, will be long known as Black Friday, for it was on that day we heard news which saddened us, which has put several local families in mourning, and has plunged others into a depth of anxiety nobody but those who have relatives on service can realise . . . We regret to report that The Lee casualties during the past few days have been very heavy.

News of the Fromelles attack and of the dead and wounded soon began to arrive at The Lee. The early reports announced the deaths of Sydney Dwight, Harry Pratt, Percy Price and Edward Sharp. Some news gave false hope which only prolonged the period of anxiety. At first it was thought that Ralph Brown, Harry Harding and Arnold Morris, while wounded, had escaped death. Within days, however, it

123

for 3 honour boards, [one with 2 panels. & the other with a single panel], the cost of which would be £2.5.0 ; & the lettering 3¾ a letter.

It was calculated that this would work at at about £6.

It was decided to obtain more information from Mr Parsons, with a view to accepting his estimate, and that the Heading of the boards should be decided settled at the next Managers' Meeting.

Thanks to auditor — It was agreed that the best thanks of the Managers be accorded Mr Gibson Harris for auditing the accounts, and that a letter should be sent

Letter to Mrs A. Brown — to Mrs Arthur Brown (Asst. Teacher) expressing the Managers' sympathy with her in the loss she had sustained, lately, through the death of her husband, Q. Serj. Major Arthur Brown, killed in action.

Care Comm.ee — Miss Lochner, the Secretary of the Care Comm.ee, had sent a letter reporting on the case of Constance Picton, aged 10, feeble minded, who had been sent to a Home at Winslow, to await a vacancy at the Stoke Park Colony, Bristol. — Amy Rutland had been an in-patient of the R. Bucks Hospl, for

An entry in the Lee Common school managers' minute book agreeing to send a letter of sympathy to Mrs Arthur Brown on the death of her husband. (*Lee Common School*)

became known that they, too, had lost their lives. Arthur Brown was at first posted as 'missing'. Confirmation of his death eventually arrived on 14 August. An entry in the Lee Common School Log Book for 14 August 1916 reads: 'Mrs. Elsie Brown, having received news of the death of her husband, was unable to attend School this morning.' It was a sad coincidence that Arthur and Elsie Brown had been married exactly one year earlier on 14 August 1915.

Canon Constantine Phipps was carrying out his onerous task of comforting those Lee families who had lost husbands or sons when news reached him of the death of his own son, Charles. Canon and Mrs Phipps's elder son, Jim, was serving in the King's Own (Liverpool) Regiment on the Somme. When Jim heard that his brother had been killed, he immediately wrote to his parents:

> I was absolutely heart-broken when I first got your letter, my darlings, but I am a bit calmer now. I know that my darling, darling Charlie is happy with God in heaven. I can't bear to think or talk about it my darlings. Of course, you know only too well how terribly I shall miss him, but I will be brave my darlings. It was God's will and what God wishes must be right and good. – How I would have liked to have died for him – but it is God's will.[1]

When Constantine Phipps heard how Sydney Damant had been killed while attempting to save Charles's life he immediately wrote to Damant's mother in Marlow:

I want to write to you to thank you for your dear son's courage, and his devotion to my beloved son, Charles Phipps. I am thankful, very thankful, to know how much my son was loved by his men – what your son, Sydney, did just proves it. But it proves, too, what a gallant, brave lad he, Sydney Damant, was. A real hero, to whom I hope the Victoria Cross is due. It is hard to write more.[2]

The Lee was still absorbing the shock of the Fromelles casualty list when it suffered another blow. Two men from Lee Common, Harry Talmer and Percy Dwight, both serving with the 1/1st Bucks Battalion, had been killed on the Somme. This meant that, over a period of only a few days, eleven men from The Lee had been killed. Two families, the Browns and the Dwights, had each lost two sons. Arnold Morris had left a wife and three children. The village was stunned. The *Bucks Examiner* described The Lee as 'a place of sorrowing'.[3]

Disturbing news was also coming in about Ivor Stewart-Liberty. On 20 July, the day after the attack at Fromelles, Geoffry Christie-Miller wrote to Ivor's wife, Evelyn. The note contained news about the attack, the death of Evelyn's brother, Charles Phipps, and about Ivor's wound:

A hurried note to tell you that the battalion was in a big attack last night and that Ivor got hit in the leg. It is a 'severe wound, but not dangerous' – that is the surgeon's report on it . . . He was leading his Company in the most gallant manner and was up against a real big thing. He did splendidly and his men followed his lead A1. I am sorry to say that all his Officers were hit, but fortunately none killed. The Regiment suffered severely in officers and men. I am sorry to say that poor Charles Phipps was killed – Poor boy, I am awfully unhappy about it. We have lost Church, Atkinson and Hudson. The Battalion did splendidly, but, alas, the gaps today make one miserable. I went back to a town 6 miles behind this afternoon and had a yarn with Ivor. He is as cheery as ever and seemed comfortable. He expects to move to the coast tomorrow, so you will soon have him back. Please excuse this hasty scrawl, but I wanted you to know all I could tell you about Ivor as quickly as possible.

In fact, Ivor Stewart-Liberty's condition deteriorated rapidly. On 24 July he was described as 'dangerously ill' – the wound had become gangrenous – and on 27 July it became necessary to amputate the left leg above the knee.[4] During the night before his operation, Ivor had a particularly vivid dream:

In his delirium, he could clearly discern his late comrades, Harold Church among them . . . rise from the depths of the stormy Channel and beckon him to join them . . . Thanks to the surgical skills of Alfred Webb-Johnson the offending limb was removed and Ivor, with his invincible recuperative powers, made a swift recovery.[5]

Ivor spent some days in the military hospital at Wimereux and was then transferred to the King Edward VII Hospital in London. By early September, he was back in The Lee.

In May 1917, almost one year after Charles Phipps's death, Canon and Mrs Phipps received a letter from the Front that must have brought back all the pain of their loss. The letter was from Lt W. Gerard Kemp, serving with the 1/8th West Yorkshire Regiment in the Laventie area. He wrote that, while patrolling in No-Man's-Land, he had come across the remains of a British officer: 'From the letters on the body I gather that they belonged to your son, Lt. (Charles) Phipps of the 2/1st Bucks.' Two months later, in July 1917, Canon Phipps received a second letter from Lt Kemp:

> When I wrote last, we were expecting to 'take over' a part of the Boche line when I found your son's body. It was owing to this expected 'taking over' that I said I hoped, in the near future, to be able to have a cross put up, but the whole scheme fell through, and we were suddenly withdrawn from the sector. I fear now we have quite lost touch with the spot. However, if ever it does happen that the place becomes 'behind our lines' I can let you know the exact spot on the map.

Lt Kemp survived the war, but there is no evidence of further communication with the Phippses.[6]

The bodies of seven of The Lee men who died at Fromelles were never recovered. The names of Arthur Brown, Sydney Dwight, Harry Harding, Arnold Morris, Charles Phipps,

In the field
May 16ᵗʰ/17.

Dear Sir,

I am writing to you with reference to several letters, which I have found in "no man's land", from which I gather they belonged to your son Lieut Phipps (2/1 Bucks?) I do not know what news you have had of him, & fear that perhaps you have never received anything official. I feel sure that you will like to know that these letters have been found. If you would like to have any further details of the circumstances under which they were found, & the place, I shall be only too pleased to do anything I can.

I am.

Yrs sincerely
W Gerard Kemp 2 Lt
8ᵗʰ West Yorks Rgt
B.E.F.

The Leeds Flag Days' Committee.

Letter dated 16 May 1917 from W. Gerard Kemp of the 8th West Yorkshire Regiment, who found the body of Lt Charles Phipps in No-Man's-Land.

The Loos Memorial for the Missing has inscribed on its walls the names of the seven men from The Lee.

Percy Price and Edward Sharp are inscribed on the Loos Memorial for the Missing.[7] Ralph Brown and Harry Pratt have their graves in the Merville Communal Cemetery.[8]

Earlier in 1916, Canon Phipps had written to his congregation: 'There is the same determined spirit everywhere . . . to see this thing through to a victorious conclusion, and towards this end we are prepared to strain every nerve and make every sacrifice.'[9] His words were proving to be prophetic for many families in The Lee. Until July 1916, only one Lee man had been killed in the war.[10] During the six-month period July–December 1916, fifteen men were killed and by the end of the war thirty Lee men had died. In addition, thirty-six men had been wounded.

On the basis that about 160 men from The Lee parish took part in the war, this represents a casualty rate of over 40 per cent.

* * *

Despite the trauma of 1916, the villagers of The Lee, supported and encouraged by the manor house, the church and the chapels, doggedly carried on. A United Service of Intercession was held in the manor gardens on 4 August 1916 to mark the second anniversary of the war. A resolution was passed:

> That this meeting of the inhabitants of The Lee, Bucks, desires to express its earnest conviction that notwithstanding the awful cost of the War in precious lives, in which The Lee has its share, it is the duty of England to persevere in the Great Struggle against German oppression and cruelty till, with God's help, complete victory is won.[11]

The established routines of the village continued. The church bell was rung every day at noon. Church and chapel services and events went on. Mrs Arthur Brown organised carol singing around the village at Christmas 1916 and raised £11 10s for the National Institute for Blind Soldiers. The event was appreciated so much that it was repeated in both 1917 and 1918. Mrs Phipps ran the lending library in the Guild Room and the parish council discussed possible gas and water supplies and the poor state of the roads, particularly Leather Lane. The ladies of the War Working Party went on with their knitting and sewing. In May 1917, in response to Queen Mary's appeal to send the troops a 'Shower of Gifts', the Working Party made a special effort and put together

a case containing 132 handkerchiefs, 29 pairs of socks, 52 items of stationery, 35 books, 18 pairs of mittens, 1 soldier's bag, 2 pairs of ward socks, about 100 picture post-cards, 8 washing swabs, 6 lavender sachets, 41 pencils, 9 games, 9 packs of playing cards, 3 woollen scarves, 3 sets of pyjamas, and 1 pair of operation stockings. Altogether 340 items.

They received a letter of thanks from Buckingham Palace.[12]

The Lee Magazine was used as a vehicle to publicise Government legislation. The regulations concerning the 'Notification of Measles and German Measles' appeared in the magazine of January 1916. The Lighting Order came into effect on 22 July 1916 in response to the threat of air raids. The August magazine carried a notice stating that 'Public lighting should be extinguished or reduced except that necessary for Safety. Domestic lighting should be shaded or reduced so that no more than a dull subdued light is visible from any direction outside.'

The unrestricted use of submarines by the Germans in 1917 harmed Britain considerably by reducing grain and other imports. Canon Phipps commented that 'our food shortage is certainly an uneasy fact owing to the piratical efforts of the Germans'.[13] The Government's Voluntary Food Restrictions came into effect in February 1917 and *The Lee Magazine* listed the suggested weekly limits: 4 lb of bread (or 3 lb of flour), 2½ lb of meat and ¾ lb of sugar. In view of the Food Restrictions, a parishioner wrote to the Food Controller asking if the 'small entertainments that have been held locally in former years viz. Sunday School Treats, Mothers' Meeting Teas, Good Friday Hot Cross Bun Distribution, etc. should be continued'. As the editor of the April 1917 magazine put it: 'The answer has come with no uncertain touch.' The Ministry of Food letter read: 'I am able to state that the Food Controller considers that in view of the necessity of conserving our national supply of food all such entertainment should discontinue.'

In June 1917 the magazine printed in full a proclamation issued by the King:

> The abstention from all unnecessary consumption of grain will furnish the surest and most effective means of defeating the devices of our enemies . . . We exhort and charge all heads of households to reduce the consumption of bread by at least one-fourth of the quantity in ordinary times; to abstain from the use of flour in pastry. In like manner we exhort and charge all persons who keep horses to abandon the practice of feeding the same on oats and other grain.

The Proclamation was read out in the church and chapels of The Lee.

With food shortages came rising prices. As a contributor to the November 1917 *Lee Magazine* observed: 'We in this country have got to make up our minds to go through more hardship than hitherto. Food is dearer and more difficult to get. Oil and coal are very dear and not likely to be any cheaper.' With commendable initiative, Mrs Fountain of Park Cottage submitted the following substitute for suet: 'Take a good size and sound potato, grate and chop very fine into some flour. Add a pinch of salt and mix.' She claimed that it would make an excellent suet pudding.

In addition to the difficulties and problems caused by food shortages and rising prices, the villagers of The Lee had to come to terms with an even more harrowing event – the arrival of the casualty list. Five local men were killed in 1917 and six in 1918. During those two years almost every edition of the magazine carried news of Lee men who had been wounded, gassed or who were missing.

1917 was particularly miserable. It was in May of that year that Sir Arthur Liberty died. *The Lee Magazine* carried an account of the funeral:

On Tuesday 13 May, it was the privilege of those of us living at or near The-Lee to assist on removing the body from the Manor to the Church. At 7.00pm the coffin was placed on a cart from Home Farm and followed by Lady Liberty and the rest of the immediate relatives, by representatives of all connected with the Estate and the Parish and by many of his servants and friends. The coffin was placed in the Chancel of the Church and after a short and impressive service by Canon Phipps it was left there to be watched over by volunteers from the Parish. The burial service was held on Wednesday 14 May at 3.15pm and was attended by some hundreds of people . . . It was a thoroughly representative gathering not only of his family, personal friends, tenants and neighbours, but there were representatives from the various Societies that he was interested in. The Service was taken by the Bishop of Buckingham and Canon Phipps and among those present were one hundred and fifty members of the Regent Street staff and over one hundred schoolchildren from The Lee.

Walter Beeson, the superintendent of the Swan Bottom chapel, spoke for everyone when he said: 'In him we lose a true, righthearted friend.' The whole parish mourned.[14]

The villagers showed amazing resilience as they dealt with their many problems, but sadness and grief were never far away. They had little option but to follow the guidance of a contributor to *The Lee Magazine*: 'Whatever betides, it is our duty to do what Englishmen have done in the past. Never despair, never own ourselves beaten, grit our teeth and see it through to the end.' And Holy Jim Pearce wrote to his congregation:

The way is long and painful, but reflection makes it clear that until Germany abandons her arrogance and promises reparation to Belgium, we dare not abandon the path we have been compelled to tread. Better a universal financial bankruptcy than a moral one. We could live in a world of severe simplicity. We could not live in one dominated by Prussianism. We must have patience because our cause is right.[15]

* * *

On 11 November 1918 the First World War came to an end. The Allies – principally France, Britain and Italy (Russia had left the war in 1917) – had finally defeated the German and Austrian forces. But peace had been gained only at great cost. An estimated total of 10 million men had died in the war. Britain had lost some 750,000 men and every city, town and village had suffered.

The news of the Armistice was received in The Lee with a mixture of relief and euphoria. In the December 1918 *Lee Magazine*, Ivor Stewart-Liberty wrote: 'It has come! Peace and Victory! We may well be proud that it has been left to our generation to rid the world forever from ambitious and murderous despotism.' When Canon Phipps heard the news he immediately went to Lee Common School. 'The Vicar said a few words, the Flag saluted, the National Anthem sung and rounds of cheers were given.' He then organised an evening service of thanksgiving: 'How can we adequately describe that wonderful assemblage of joyful people in our little Church at 7.00pm. Everyone who could be was in attendance and right gladly did we sing.'

At a meeting of the parish council on 21 November 1918 the following motion was proposed:

The Lee Parish Council on the occasion of its first meeting since the cessation of hostilities reverently salutes those who have given their lives for their Country's Great Cause and tender its sympathy to the bereaved; the Council is proud of the active and patriotic part played by the sons and daughters of the Parish in bringing the War to a victorious and righteous end and thank and congratulate them one and all.

The council rose to its feet and carried the motion unanimously.

The Lee, like hundreds of other villages in Britain, did what it could to return to a normal way of life. It was natural to look back to the days before the war. As one parishioner wrote in *The Lee Magazine* of January 1919: 'What a fine thing it is to feel ourselves now in a position to think of going back to those jolly days.' As was traditional in The Lee, both the manor house and the vicarage took the initiative in guiding the village into its postwar life. A Peace Club was formed 'to assist cottagers in The-Lee Parish to purchase, at as cheap a rate as possible, and on an instalment system, Coal, Pigs, Bees, Pig and Bee food, Poultry and Poultry food, Potatoes, Vegetable and Flower seeds, Manure and Agricultural appliances . . . profits arising from the Club would be divided among the members'. Forty parishioners joined the Club at its first meeting.[16] The Lee played its first postwar cricket match on 17 May 1919 against Hyde Heath. The last time these two teams had faced one another was on 1 August 1914 – three days before war was declared. The Peace Day celebrations of 19 July included a lunch for all the ex-servicemen, a skittles competition, sports events, a tug of war, a dance and fireworks. The School Treat took place on 23 July and the football and rifle clubs started up in Autumn 1919. Canon Phipps wrote:

> I should dearly love to see some such movement to that of the Boy Scouts initiated in the Parish . . . Then there are the girls. They too ought to have some sort of a Club or Society which would be the means of bringing them together for purposes of recreation and intellectual and spiritual improvement . . . And what about my suggestion as to a Village Glee Club or Choral Society? Anyhow, I am most anxious for brighter and better days to come, when we might strive together to do what we can, in a social way, to bring the light of progress and happiness into the lives of those around us, and to make village life the joy it ought to be.[17]

Despite the great efforts to recapture the past, it was clear that things would never be quite the same again. There had been too much grief. The 'Golden Age' of The Lee – the ten years or so before the start of the war – was a world away. The 'Lee Weeks' of that period, when Sir Arthur and Lady Liberty and Ivor Stewart-Liberty had entertained their friends at the manor with tennis, cricket, billiards, singing, drinks and dancing, were just distant memories. They were never repeated. Too many of the Liberty circle had died in the years since the last Lee Week in 1914. Too many village families had suffered.

Ivor Stewart-Liberty's personal scrapbook contains photographs of his friends from Oxford and The Lee. Many of them are of young men in army uniforms and, frequently, alongside these pictures, in Ivor's handwriting, are the dates of their death in the war. Capt Edward Shaw, the son of the Bishop of Oxford, died in France in 1916. Mark Philips, Ivor's friend from Oxford and a frequent guest at The Lee Weeks, was killed in 1917. Evelyn Stewart-Liberty's brother-in-law, Lionel Crouch, from Aylesbury, lost his life just two days after the Fromelles attack, at Pozières on the Somme. A photograph taken at the wedding of Ivor Stewart-Liberty and Evelyn Phipps in 1913 has on it six men, all of whom had good reason to believe that the future had everything to offer. But events decided otherwise. Sir Arthur Liberty died in 1917 after a long period of illness. Charles Phipps was killed at Fromelles. His brother, Jim Phipps, who had won both the Military Cross and the Distinguished Service Order, survived the war only to die of influenza in 1919 while still in Germany. Canon Constantine Phipps never recovered from the death of his two sons and he himself died, it is said of a broken heart, in 1921. Ivor's best man, Spencer Thomson, another Oxford friend, served with the Durham Light Infantry in Gallipoli and then in France where he was killed in 1917. Of the men in the photograph, only Ivor survived – even though severely disabled.

But there were those of the Liberty circle who came through the war and continued their contact with The Lee. Teulon

The wedding of Evelyn Phipps and Ivor Stewart-Liberty, October 1913. The men on this photograph are, left to right: Sir Arthur Liberty, Canon Constantine Phipps, Charles Phipps, Ivor Stewart-Liberty, Jim Phipps and Spencer Thomson.

Sonnenschien, who had changed his name to Stallybrass in 1917, was a regular visitor to The Lee both before and after the war. Poor eye-sight had kept him out of the armed forces and he spent the war as a civil servant dealing with munitions. After the war, Stallybrass continued his academic career and eventually became principal of Brasenose College. In 1947 he was appointed vice chancellor of Oxford University. One year later, he was found dead on the railway line near Iver. It was thought that, as a consequence of his bad eye-sight, he had fallen from the carriage of the train.

G.D. 'Khaki' Roberts, sportsman and lawyer, had started the war in the 8th Devons and had seen active service in France. In 1915, he was transferred to carry out legal work in the adjutant general's branch. It was a move which, he claimed, undoubtedly saved his life.[18] After the war, Khaki developed a reputation as an aggressive prosecutor in murder cases. He reached the pinnacle of his career as a member of the prosecuting team at the Nuremberg War Trials in 1946 where he was described as 'a large man swathed in yards of double-breasted serge . . . He had a large mouth and large square teeth that he flashed at his prey in exuberant contempt.'[19] In the years following the First World War, Khaki visited The Lee on many occasions, often turning out for the village cricket team.

Ashley 'Budgie' Cummins also survived the war. The training course that he attended in July 1916 meant that by good fortune he missed the disastrous attack at Fromelles. But Budgie had not been in the best of health for some time and the Army Medical Board diagnosed rheumatic fever, anaemia and signs of a heart disorder – all brought on by 'active service conditions'. After a period of convalescence in England, Budgie was appointed a courts martial officer in Ireland, but he returned to France in 1918. In 1921, Budgie married Ivor Stewart-Liberty's sister Mary. He worked after the war for the Dock and Harbour Authorities Association and lived in The Lee for many years. He took an active part in local affairs and became chairman of the parish council and a JP. He also continued to write his poetry, many examples of which appeared in *The Lee Magazine*. In early 1923, Ivor Stewart-Liberty presented the village with a captured German field-gun which was duly sited on the Green. Budgie marked the occasion with a verse:

> Who Stole my gun?
> Said the Hun.
> It was moulded in Essen
> To teach foes a lesson.
> And Britain was one.
>
> Who could it be?
> Said The Lee.
> But the men of our village,
> Called up from the tillage
> To keep England free.

Ashley 'Budgie' Cummins died in 1972 aged eighty-five.

* * *

When Sir Arthur Liberty died in 1917, Ivor took over many of Sir Arthur's responsibilities. He became chairman of Liberty's in London and the lord of the manor at The Lee. He immersed himself in village and county life. He became chairman of the parish council, a churchwarden, editor of *The Lee Magazine*, a school manager, a Buckingham county councillor, a high sheriff and a deputy lieutenant of the county.

However, it seemed as though memories of the war and of the 2/1st Bucks were never far from Ivor's mind. He helped his Fromelles ex-comrades where he could. Sgt Joseph Petty, who had saved Ivor's life, was employed at the Liberty shop in London. Wally Delderfield, who had been a sergeant in Ivor's company, became an estate gamekeeper and was provided with a cottage in Field End Lane. Ivor helped the family of Arnold Morris, his batman, who had been killed at Fromelles. Returning soldiers went back to their old jobs on the estate – mainly agricultural.

The minutes of the Lee Common school managers' meeting of February 1917 contain an echo of the attack at Fromelles which was consistent with Ivor Stewart-Liberty's memories of the war and his whimsical sense of humour. The school had started a pig club. The children each contributed 6*d* towards the purchase of two piglets, which, when sufficiently fattened, were sold and the profit distributed among the children. In February 1917 two piglets were bought and the managers, of whom Ivor was one, named one of them 'Rhondda' and the other one 'Yap'. The name of the trench through which the 2/1st Bucks moved into No-Man's-Land at Fromelles was called 'Rhondda Sap' – a curious rhyming similarity with the names of the piglets.

The 2/1st Bucks Battalion remained one of Ivor Stewart-Liberty's main interests. After the attack at Fromelles, the Battalion was brought up to strength – mainly by drafts from outside the county – and moved to the Somme area. It was involved in the fighting in the St-Quentin sector and also at Ypres. It was at St-Julien, near Ypres, in August 1917, that the Battalion suffered losses that were equivalent to those at Fromelles. Of the 650 men who took part in the attack, 349 became casualties. The only remaining Lee man in the 2/1st Bucks, Joe Pratt, was wounded and captured in that attack. He spent the remainder of the war as a prisoner in Germany.

In early 1918, because of a manpower shortage, the brigade structure of the British Army was altered: there were to be three battalions per brigade instead of four. It was as a consequence of this change that the 2/1st Bucks Battalion was disbanded and amalgamated with the 2/4th Ox and Bucks Light Infantry. There were, naturally, regrets among the Bucks men at the loss of the county identity. However, the amalgamation went ahead smoothly – helped, probably, because at that stage in the war the proportion of Bucks men in the Battalion had reduced considerably.[20]

After the war, Ivor Stewart-Liberty became a prime mover in forming the 2/1st Bucks Old Comrades' Association. The main event was the annual church service in St Mary's, Aylesbury, followed by a lunch – paid for by the officers. This reunion continued well into the 1930s.

Maj Geoffry Christie-Miller, the second in command of the Battalion at the time of Fromelles, survived the war winning the Military Cross and the Distinguished Service Order. He regularly attended at the 2/1st Bucks reunions and he took it upon himself to press for an official recognition of the part played by the Battalion during the war. He also believed that the Fromelles attack was of sufficient importance to merit a battle honour – a recognition it had been studiously denied. Christie-Miller was not alone in this view. Lt Col A.V. Spencer DSO, of the 2nd Battalion, Ox and Bucks, wrote of Fromelles:

This action was at the time overshadowed by the Battle of the Somme and for this reason has perhaps been omitted from the battle honours hitherto given, but it would seem to be of sufficient magnitude to merit the award of a separate battle honour. It is true that the attacking troops did not succeed in holding the ground they gained, but that was the case in several other battles which have been authorised to be carried on Colours, for instance Aubers of May 1915.[21]

Christie-Miller made repeated attempts to gain a battle honour for Fromelles, but he was unsuccessful. It was of some consolation, however, that Christie-Miller, working with the County Territorial Force Association, was instrumental in persuading the War Office to compose 'a brief statement of the services rendered to the Country during hostilities by the 2/1(T.F.) Bucks Battalion'.[22] The statement outlined the history of the 2/1st Bucks and included the sentence: 'In every engagement in which this Battalion took part it upheld the brilliant and glorious traditions of the Oxford and Buckinghamshire Light Infantry to which it belonged.' The statement also refers to the attack at Fromelles: '[The Battalion] took part in the attack of 19 July on the German positions at the foot of the Aubers Ridge, receiving praise for its conduct from the Brigadier.'

* * *

Gradually, the servicemen of The Lee were demobilised. In January 1919 Joe Pratt and Leonard Keen returned from Germany where they had been prisoners of war. In February Alf Brown, Harry Chandler, George Chapman, Stanley Hearn, Charles Jennings, Alf Langstone, Harry Lewington, David Pearce, Frank Pratt and Alfred Talmer were among the first to be demobilised. By the end of March, over twenty Lee men had returned home and the process continued for the next few months. The men returned to their jobs and according to *The Lee Magazine* of March 1919: 'They settled into civilian life once again.'

On his return home, Joe Pratt, like many of his contemporaries, spoke little about his war experiences or of his life as a prisoner. In 1920 he married his childhood girlfriend, Dolly Pearce. They had one child, a daughter. Joe took up his old farming job at Bassibones Farm, but several years later he became an employee of the local council working on road maintenance. He led a quiet life spending his spare time in his allotment or on his hobby of mending clocks. Joe and Dolly never moved from Lee Common and Joe died there in 1976 aged eighty-one.

It was inevitable that the process of 'settling into civilian life' would prove difficult for many soldiers – the horrors and violence that they had witnessed must have left their mark. However, there is no particular indication that these problems surfaced among the returning soldiers of The Lee – though there was one notable and tragic exception. In November 1919 a particularly distressing event concerning an ex-soldier shocked The Lee. The headline in the *Bucks*

Examiner of 5 December 1919 read: 'The Saddest of All Tales.' Harry Channer, the son of Arthur and Marcy Channer of Lee Common, had joined the Coldstream Guards in 1915. However, after only a few months' training at the Caterham depot, he was involved in a serious accident which resulted in the amputation of his left foot. He also had severe damage to his head including concussion and was unconscious for three days. As the newspaper report said: 'There are some who think that the head injury left its effects.'

Harry Channer, after a period of convalescence, was invalided out of the Army and took up work as a labourer. One of his cousins was Kate Bignall, whose parents also lived in Lee Common, and, in 1916 Harry and Kate became engaged. Kate worked as a domestic servant at Springfield Grange in Potter Row and Harry's sister, Minnie, worked there with her. They were close friends.

In the autumn of 1919 there had been some friction between Kate and Harry – it is said because Kate objected to Harry's gambling habits – and Kate broke off the engagement on 16 November. One week later, on Sunday 23 November, Harry went with his sister, Minnie, to the morning service at Great Missenden church. Kate remained on duty in Springfield Grange. The Sunday evening was dark and stormy and Harry accompanied Minnie back to Springfield Grange. Through Minnie, Harry asked Kate to meet him outside the house. Kate agreed to this and went out into the garden. Almost immediately, Minnie, who had remained indoors, heard 'loud and piercing screams'. She rushed outside and there found Kate 'with an awful gash in her throat, the wound extended right across the throat'. Help was summoned and Harry was found, also with his throat slashed, a few yards away from Kate. A bloodstained razor was found under Harry's body.

Minnie – the sister of one victim and the cousin of the other – was clearly overcome and in her grief threw herself down a small well in the garden. The water in the well was some 17 feet deep and when Minnie's body was recovered she too was found to be dead. Kate Bignall and Minnie Channer were buried in the parish churchyard on Wednesday 26 November. In the margin of the burial register, against Kate Bignall's name, Canon Phipps wrote: 'Murdered foully'.

* * *

Even before the end of the war, the people of The Lee were discussing the idea of a memorial for those who had lost their lives. The discussion was opened in the February 1918 *Lee Magazine*:

> The time is not very far distant, we hope, when this great and appalling war will be over. When we have secured that peace, for which many have fought, doubtless we shall be anxious to do something to mark our pride in these men and to ensure that, not only we but our children and our children's children shall have a perpetual and constant memorial of those who battled for us in these the saddest and the proudest days of our history.

The article ended: 'Correspondence on this subject will be welcome.' This invitation was eagerly taken up by the villagers and the debate continued for a further eighteen months.

Canon Phipps was the first to come up with a suggestion: 'To my mind there is only one sort of Memorial which is likely to satisfy most people, and that is the Restoration of our ancient Parish Church (the Old Church), with a Memorial tablet set up in it to those who have so heroically and generously made the supreme sacrifice for us.' Canon Phipps cited the Bishops of Oxford and Buckingham as supporting this proposal.

Canon Phipps's proposal, however, did not appeal to James Pearce, the leader of the Lee Clump Baptists: 'Such a distinctly Anglican idea makes no appeal to the practical live Non-Conformist mind . . . I should like to propose a small monument, very plain without any symbol or idol, such as a cross or a crucifix, with all the names [of the fallen] inscribed.' He was opposed to any

> suggestion of a shrine, as these shrines, which are being put up all over the country and blessed by Bishops and worshipped by men, women and children, are a great grief to the Protestant part of the Church of England and to Non-Conformists of our beloved country and are greatly widening the breach between Church and Dissent.

Ivor Stewart-Libery, the editor of *The Lee Magazine*, attempted to calm the Church–Dissenter issue by com-

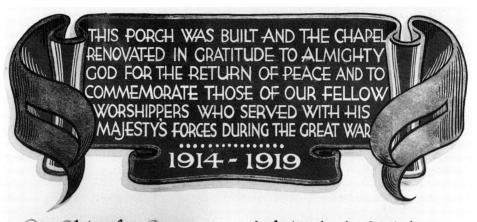

THIS PORCH WAS BUILT AND THE CHAPEL RENOVATED IN GRATITUDE TO ALMIGHTY GOD FOR THE RETURN OF PEACE AND TO COMMEMORATE THOSE OF OUR FELLOW WORSHIPPERS WHO SERVED WITH HIS MAJESTY'S FORCES DURING THE GREAT WAR

1914 - 1919

Pte. Christopher Picton.   Oxford & Bucks Lt. Infantry. Killed. Aug. 22nd 1917.

Pte. Harry Pratt.   Oxford & Bucks Lt. Infantry. Died of Wounds. July. 10th 1916.

Driver Edward Rodwell.   Royal Field Artillery. Died. Mar. 4th 1917.

Pte. Harry Talmer.   Oxford & Bucks Lt. Infantry Killed. July. 21st 1916.

Pte. Charles Talmer.   Machine Gun Corps. Died of Wounds. Sept. 24th 1916.

Gunner Joseph Hance.   Royal Garrison Artillery.

Lce. Cpl. Walter Hance.   Royal Engineers.

Pte. Leonard Keen.   Gloucesters. Prisoner of War. Apr. 26th/18.

Pte. Maurice Parsons.   Royal Warwicks. Wounded. Sept. 4th/18.

Pte. Joseph Pratt.   Oxford & Bucks Lt. Infantry. Wounded & Prisoner of War. Aug. 24th/17.

Pte. Frank Pratt.   Kings Royal Rifles. Gassed. June. 20th/18.

Pte. Harry Pearce.   Canadian Engineers.

Pte. Joseph Pearce.   Army Service Corps. Motor Transport.

Sgt. David Pearce.   Royal Field Artillery. Wounded. Sept. 21st/17.

Pte. Robert Rodwell.   Hampshire Regiment.

Pte. Alfred Talmer.   Hampshire Regiment.

The Baptists of Lee Clump placed a plaque in the porch of their chapel showing the names of the men who had fought in the war. (*Westminster City Archives*) menting: 'An essentially Church or Chapel Memorial would be most unsatisfactory. This is a sacred question – our men have fought and died together. Let us commemorate them as they died.' Nevertheless, the Baptists decided to have their own memorial in addition to whatever else was decided in The Lee.

In May 1918, Dorothea Coke of Sly Corner wrote: 'What I want to see will be a great living National Monument, educational, which will be a living thing for perpetuity: colleges for children . . . why not have colleges for the Great Dead?' The following month, Helen Keys of Ballinger proposed: 'Some structure in marble, very simple and good, with space enough on it for all the names [of the dead] cast in letters of gold. Let it be in the open – say on The Lee Green – and let there be a flower-bed in front of it and a seat nearby.' Mabel Lloyd of The Lee suggested that a bed should be endowed at the Royal Bucks Hospital in Aylesbury to be called 'The Lee Bed'. Gertrude Lockey, Lady Liberty's companion, was of the opinion that a drinking fountain should be erected on the green 'in stone, for passers-by, and a trough for animals (provided that water can be obtained) with the names of the Fallen engraved thereon'. However, when Miss Lockey heard of the idea of a 'Lee Bed' in Aylesbury Hospital, she graciously withdrew her drinking fountain scheme.

Ivor Stewart-Liberty's own proposal was ambitious:

I would suggest a dignified and appropriate Gateway connecting the Guild Room with the Old Lodge . . . On the walls of the Gateway should be inscribed the names of each soldier who had died . . . and above it there might be a small room which could be used as a War Museum and Record Room . . . In addition, we should institute the happy custom whereby every parishioner when passing through the Gateway should touch his hat or bow.

Other suggestions were almshouses and cottages for disabled parishioners. But, in the end, it was Lady Liberty's voice that prevailed: 'Lady Liberty suggested that the Memorial should be a Celtic Cross, standing on a large base, with the names of those men belonging to the Parish who had fallen inscribed thereon. Lady Liberty produced a sketch for inspection and offered to contribute £50 if the suggestion was adopted.' A public meeting in June 1919 took up Lady Liberty's proposal: 'the Cross to be placed on the village Green, a piece of land given to the Parish by Lady Liberty for that purpose'. The total cost of erecting The Lee War Memorial was £350 and all, apart from Lady Liberty's donation, was subscribed by local people.[23]

* * *

There are a number of reminders of the First World War both in Fromelles and in The Lee. Within 3 miles of Fromelles are no fewer than twenty war cemeteries. The fields around Fromelles are dotted with the remains of German concrete bunkers which roughly follow the 1916 front line. The trench systems are now no longer evident, but it is possible to pace out key positions including the Sugar Loaf salient and Wick salient and stare in awe at the flat fields across which the British and Australian troops attacked on 19 July 1916. The River Laies continues to be the main drainage channel between the Rue Tilleloy and Rue Deleval. Almost ninety years after the Fromelles attack it is still possible to find a profusion of shell cases, rusting screw picquets and shrapnel bullets. When the autumn ploughing takes place around the Sugar Loaf the exposed shrapnel bullets glint in the weak sunlight. They can be collected in handfuls.

The plaque on the wall of the *mairie* (town hall) in Fromelles commemorates the Battle of Fromelles.

IN DIESEM QUAR- -TIER LAG 1916
UNSER FUEHRER
ADOLF HITLER
ALS SOLDAT
DES BAYR. JNF. RGT. LIST
TECHN. ABT. IX 20. 4. 1942

This concrete tablet was placed on the wall of Hitler's billet in Fournes-en-Weppes in 1942 and was broken off the wall when France was liberated.

The town square in Fromelles is dedicated to the attack of 19 July 1916. In 1989, a group of local men, interested in the First World War, formed the 'Association pour le Souvenir de la Bataille de Fromelles' (ASBF) and put together a museum of British, Australian and German war artefacts found in the area. The museum is housed in the Fromelles town hall.

One particularly interesting item in the museum, a sidelight on the Fromelles attack, is a pieced-together concrete tablet inscribed: 'Our Fuhrer, Adolf Hitler, was here in 1916 – a soldier in the Bavarian List Infantry Regiment.' It was the List Regiment – the 16th Bavarian

Reserve – that had defended the Sugar Loaf against the 2/1st Bucks Battalion at Fromelles. There is no evidence that Hitler was in the front line during the Fromelles attack, but he was certainly billeted at that time in Fournes-en-Weppes, a hamlet about 4 miles east of Fromelles. The concrete tablet was placed on the wall of Hitler's 1916 billet when the Fuhrer visited the area in 1942. It was hacked off the wall and broken into pieces when Fournes was liberated.

* * *

The 61st Division plaque was placed on the wall of the *mairie* at Laventie in 1935.

Apart from the Commonwealth War Graves Commission headstones and the names on memorials commemorating individual soldiers,[24] there is no monument in France to the 2/1st Bucks recording their part in the attack at Fromelles. In fact, there is no monument to any of the British battalions who took part in that attack. The only general reminder of British presence in that area is a plaque on the wall of the town hall in Laventie. The plaque was unveiled there in 1935 by Sir Colin Mackenzie, the 61st Division commander at the time of Fromelles. It reads: 'This tablet was erected by the British 61st Division to commemorate fallen comrades. The Division first served during the Great War in the neighbourhood of this town of Laventie and is proud to leave its dead sleeping in the sacred soil of France.' The tablet has on it the 61st Division emblem and the cap-badges of the battalions who had fought in the Laventie area, including that of the 2/1st Bucks.

The Australian memorials at Fromelles are far more imposing. On the Rue Delvas, at a point just in front of the Australian 1916 front line, there now stands a cemetery known as VC Corner.[25] It is the only all-Australian cemetery in France and on the walls of the memorial are the names of 1,298 Australians who were declared 'missing' or unidentified after the Fromelles attack. Close to VC Corner is the Australian Memorial Park. The park has in it the remains of German concrete bunkers and the bronze sculpture *Cobbers*.[26] The sculpture commemorates the bravery of the Australian soldiers who brought in the wounded from No-Man's-Land and, in particular, it represents Sgt Simon Fraser

VC Corner stands on the 1916 Australian front line. It is the only all-Australian cemetery in France.

rescuing a comrade of the 60th Australian Battalion. On the base is a plaque with the words: 'In memory of those who fought and fell in the Battle of Fromelles 19/20 July 1916'. The plaque also quotes Sgt Fraser: 'for the next three days we did great work getting in the wounded from the front and I must say [the Germans] treated us fairly . . . we must have brought in 250 men by our Company alone.'

* * *

The appearance of The Lee is very much as it was at the time of the First World War. The oak trees planted by Sir Arthur Liberty still line the roads leading into the village. The Cock and Rabbit, the Guild Room, Miss Stone's post office, the Old and New Vicarages, the school at Lee Common, the Old

Swan at Swan Bottom and The-Lee Manor can all be easily identified. St John the Baptist continues to be the parish church and the 'Old Church', in the same churchyard, is used for occasional services and social gatherings. The Lee Common Methodist chapel is still in use.

Services are no longer held in the Emmanuel chapel in Swan Bottom. The Lee Clump Baptist chapel is now a private house, though the tombstones, including those of 'Holy' Joe Pearce and of Joe and Dolly Pratt, remain in the garden. Lee Common, Lee Clump, Swan Bottom, Hunts Green and King's Ash are also very much as they were –

The bronze sculpture *Cobbers* by Peter Corlett at the Australian Memorial.

though some additional houses have been built and, along Oxford Street, Mr and Mrs Lewington's store, among others, has gone. Lady Liberty built 'Peace Cottages' after the war and these can be found in Swan Bottom and Lee Common.

Along Field End Lane, towards Ballinger, is a simple wooden seat. It is marked in memory of Emily Morris and her two daughters, Norah and Margaret. It is said that this was Emily's favourite spot – the place where she waved a last farewell to her husband, Arnold, gamekeeper turned soldier, as he set off for France in May 1916.

The parish church of St John the Baptist is full of reminders of the First World War. A Book of Remembrance recording the names of the fallen of The Lee is on permanent display. The original wooden cross that once marked the grave of Jim Phipps in Germany now hangs inside the church. Just before he died, Canon Phipps presented an altar cross and two candlesticks in memory of his two sons, Jim and Charles. The cross is still on the altar, but the two candlesticks were stolen in 1973. Canon Phipps's grave is immediately outside the vestry door and, inside the church, on the choir wall, is a commemoration plaque with the words: 'He Was The Father Of His People And Little Children Loved Him'.

Capt Arthur Liberty Millar, Sir Arthur and Lady Liberty's nephew who died in Salonika in 1918, has a marble memorial in the south transept. Also in the church is a stained-glass window and a brass plaque in memory of a young airman, Cyril Arthur Duxford, who died on active service in May 1918. Cyril Duxford, not a local boy, was the nephew of Mrs Brodie Keyl of Ballinger.

The Liberty family vault in the churchyard contains the graves of Sir Arthur and Lady Liberty and those of Evelyn and Ivor Stewart-Liberty and members of their family. Ralph Rodwell and Charles Talmer have their official War Graves Commission headstones in the churchyard.[27]

The most impressive of the reminders of the war is The Lee War Memorial on the village green which bears the names of The Lee dead and is inscribed: 'To the Glory of God and in Memory of these Men from The Lee who gave their Lives for King, Country, Hearth and Home, Freedom and Honour in Britain's War against German Cruelty and Aggression'. A brass plate on the memorial step, commemorating the 85th anniversary of the attack at Fromelles, has the words: 'Nine men from this village were slain at Fromelles in northern France on 19 July 1916. Their names are recorded on this War Memorial and soil from their graves in France was brought back in 2001 and buried beneath this plaque in honour and remembrance of their gallantry and sacrifice.'

The deaths at Fromelles were among the first of the war that directly affected The Lee and the relative size of the loss was traumatic for the whole parish. The experience of the attack at Fromelles and its consequences was a story repeated many times during the First World War, of ordinary men carrying out an impossible task with extraordinary gallantry. In Ivor Stewart-Liberty's words they were indeed 'the saddest and the proudest days'.[28]

APPENDIX A

Particulars of the Thirty Men whose Names are Carved on The Lee War Memorial

From The Lee Magazine of January 1921

EDGAR GERALD ADAMS. – The son of Thomas and Annie Adams of Rabbs Corner. He enlisted in August 1914 in the Grenadier Guards and was soon in France. He was home for a time with 'trench feet'. Soon after his return to France he was reported missing after an attack on 15 September 1916.

ARTHUR BROWN. – The husband of Elsie Brown and fourth son of William Harry and Leah Brown of Lee Common. He enlisted in August 1914 in the London Regiment, but transferred the following month to the 2nd Bucks Battalion. He, like his elder brother Ralph, gained rapid promotion and was Sergeant Major of Captain Church's Company when the Battalion crossed to France. He was killed, by the side of his Company Commander, a few minutes after 6 o'clock in the evening of the 19 July, 1916, during an attack on the German lines near Laventie. Had he lived, he would have been recommended for special distinction, not only for his splendid work on the day of his death, but also for his great bravery during a gas explosion on the previous day.

RALPH WILLIAM BROWN. – The third son of William Harry and Leah Brown of Ivy Cottage, Lee Common. He enlisted in November 1914 in the 2nd Bucks Battalion. He gained rapid promotion and crossed to France with his Battalion as Company Sergeant Major in Captain Stewart-Liberty's Company. He was hit in the stomach by a machine gun bullet during an attack on the German lines near Laventie, soon after 6 p.m. on the 19 July 1916.

He died from his wounds the following day at Merville, where he lies buried. Had he lived, Colonel H.M. Williams, V.D., had intended recommending him for the D.C.M.

FRANK CHANNER. – The husband of Elizabeth Channer and third son of Arthur and Mary Jane Channer of Lee Common. He served through the war as a Stoker in His Majesty's Navy (H.M.S. *Vanguard*, etc.) and was drowned at sea in April 1919 whilst engaged on mine sweeping.

HAROLD CLARK. – The third son of Harry and Margaret Clark of Church Farm. He enlisted in the Royal Dragoons in May 1917 and went on service to France with the 8th Battalion of the Leicester Regiment. He was reported missing as from 22 March 1918.

GEORGE DORRELL. – The son of James and Elizabeth Dorrell of King's Ash. He enlisted in Australia, where he was working before the war, in September 1915 in the 31st Battalion, Australian Imperial Force. He died on the 15th December 1916 from wounds received in action on the Somme.

PERCY DWIGHT. – The second son of Jesse and Lydia Dwight of Lee Common. He enlisted in December 1914 in the 1st Bucks Battalion and went to France in the Summer of 1915. He was killed on 15 August 1916 during the Battle of the Somme.

SYDNEY DWIGHT. – The fourth son of Jesse and Lydia Dwight of Lee Common. He enlisted in January 1915 in the 2nd Bucks Battalion. He served in Captain Stewart-Liberty's Company and was killed on the evening of the 19 July during an attack on the German lines near Laventie.

HARRY HARDING. – The husband of Rose Hannah Harding of Kingswood, the second son of Samuel and Martha Harding of Corner Wood. He was in the Bucks Territorials before the war and went with the 1st Battalion to France in April 1915 where he was wounded in the thigh and returned home. Later, he left for Salonika and was reported missing as from 9 May 1917 whilst serving on that front. Besides a widow, he leaves his son Ronald.

HARRY HARDING. – The son of Thomas and Amelia Harding of Furze Field Lane, Swan Bottom. He enlisted in November 1915 in the 2nd Bucks Battalion and took part in the attack on the German lines near Laventie on 19 July 1916 when he was taken prisoner and, it is believed, wounded. He died on or after the 19th while a prisoner of war.

FREDERICK HEARN. – The third son of Frederick William and Sarah Hearn of Dell Cottage, Lee Common. He enlisted in January 1915 in the C/187th Brigade, Royal Field Artillery. He died of wounds received in action 20 May 1918. His Major, in writing to his mother, said, 'No matter what was going on, he was always an example to us of duty, well done with a good heart and cheerfulness, which helped more than one of us on our way.'

GEORGE HEARN. – The son of Daniel and Elizabeth Hearn of Corner Wood. He enlisted in March 1916 in the 7th Royal West Kents and went on service to France. He died from acute bronchitis on 29 November 1918 at No. 12 Casualty Clearing Station. He lies buried in Busigny in France.

GEORGE HENRY HEARN. – The son of Frederick and Sarah Hearn of Dell Cottage, Lee Common. He enlisted in November 1916 in the 13th Battalion Middlesex Regiment, and afterwards transferred to the Royal Fusiliers. He was taken prisoner and after being in captivity for 17 months he died in Germany, in September 1918.

WILLIAM MARCHAM. – The husband of Mary Marcham and second son of Frederick and Ellen Marcham of The Manor Lodge, The-Lee. He was one of the first Lee men to enlist and joined the 6th Battalion O. & B. L.I. in August 1914, but at the time of his death, he was with the 1/6th Battalion of the West Yorks Regiment. He was First wounded on 25 September 1915 at the Battle of Loos, again on 12 February 1916 at Ypres, again on 7 October in the same year at Guesdecourt, and again on 20 September 1917 at Menin Road. Finally he was wounded on 8 August 1918 (the day of Britain's great offensive), and from the results of these wounds, died at 10 a.m. on 13 August 1918 at 10 Casualty Station in France. He was in his 25th year and, besides his widow, he leaves a son, Donald.

ARNOLD WILLIAM MORRIS. – The husband of Emily Lydia Morris, of Field End, and son of William and Phoebe Morris of Knightwick, near Worcester. He enlisted in February 1915 in the 2nd Bucks Battalion and soon qualified as a Scout (1st Class). He was offered promotion, but loyally decided to remain Captain Stewart-Liberty's 'batman'. He was killed on the evening of 19 July 1916 during an attack on the German lines near Laventie. Besides a widow, he left three children, Arthur William, Margaret Edith, and Norah Madeline.

JOHN THOMAS PEARCE. – The son of William and Elizabeth Pearce of Swan Bottom. He was a Reservist and joined the 2nd Battalion of the O. & B. L.I. in September 1914. He crossed to France with the 2nd Division; was reported missing after the Battle of Festubert and concluded killed on 16 May 1915. He was born on 2 October 1874.

ALBERT PHILLIPS. – The husband of Rose Phillips, and the son of George and Louisa Phillips of Prestwood. He enlisted in February 1916 in the 17th London Cyclists Corps and soon afterwards transferred to the King's (Liverpool) Regiment. He was killed on 17 September 1917 by a sniper's bullet whilst doing his turn as forward sentry. A tree from The-Lee Manor Gardens has been planted on his grave, which is in the garden of the Chateau at Kemmel.

CHARLES PERCY PHIPPS. – The second son of the Rev. Constantine Osborne and Mabel Phipps of The-Lee Vicarage. He was given a commission in the 2nd Bucks Battalion in September 1914 and crossed to France with the Battalion as a Lieutenant. During an attack on the German lines near Laventie, on the evening of 19 July 1916, he was at the head of his platoon when a bullet broke his leg. His servant, Damant, of Marlow, lifted him up and tried to regain the British lines, when machine gun fire killed them both. He was educated at Cordwallis School, Maidenhead, and at Winchester College, and was in his 21st year when he died.

CONSTANTINE JAMES PHIPPS, D.S.O., M.C. – The eldest son of The Rev. Canon Constantine Osborne and Mabel Phipps, of The-Lee Vicarage. At the outbreak of the War he was a 2nd Lieutenant in the 1st Battalion of The

King's (Liverpool) Regiment and crossed to France with that battalion on 12 August 1914. He was wounded in the foot on the retreat from Mons. He soon rejoined his Regiment and was again wounded, this time in the chest, on 3 March 1915 near Givenchy. He gained the D.S.O. in January 1919, and the M.C. in January 1916 and was mentioned in dispatches three times, in 1915, 1917, 1918. During 1916 he was attached to the R.E. as a signalling officer and by 1918 he was a Major (one of the youngest in the British Army) and the Officer Commanding the 2nd Signal Company, R.E., with the 2nd Division. Having served throughout the whole war with very exceptional brilliancy, he died of influenza and pneumonia at Duren, near Cologne, on 19 February 1919. His grave is in the cemetery at Duren. He was educated at Cordwallis School, Maidenhead, and at Winchester.

CHRISTOPHER PICTON. – The third son of Thomas and Annie Picton of Lee Common. He enlisted in October 1916 in the O. & B. L.I. and was killed at Ypres on 22 August 1917.

HARRY PRATT. – The second son of George and Ellen Pratt of Lee Common. He enlisted in December 1915 in the 2nd Bucks Battalion and crossed to France in May 1916. He died from wounds (the same shell wounded his brother Joseph) received in the front line in the Ferme du Bois Sector on 10 July 1916.

PERCY ALLEN PRICE. – The son of Albert G. and S.H. Price of 'The Swan', Swan Bottom. He enlisted in November 1915 in the 2nd Bucks Battalion. He was killed 19 July 1916 in an attack on the German lines near Laventie.

HAROLD RICHARD RODWELL. – The husband of Ivy Rodwell and eldest son of Joseph and Jane Rodwell. He enlisted in May 1916 in the Royal West Kent Regiment and saw service in France and Belgium. After an attack in the neighbourhood of Dickybush on 21 September 1917 he was reported missing, and afterwards as killed, on that date.

RALPH RODWELL. – The second son of Joseph and Jane Rodwell of 'Fairholme', Lee Common. He enlisted in July 1916 in the 9th Battalion O. & B.

L.I. and died from meningitis at Tiverton on 26 December 1916. He is buried in The-Lee Churchyard.

ALBERT RUTLAND. – The third son of Alfred and Ellen Rutland of The-Lee. He enlisted in December 1915 (having tried to do so a year previously) in the 2nd Bucks Battalion. He took part, unharmed, in the battle near Laventie on 19 July 1916 when so many of his Lee comrades lost their lives. He died 27 March 1917 at the 8th General Hospital, Rouen, from nephritis and is buried at Boisguillaume near that city.

EDWARD SHARP. – The second son of Alfred and Jane Sharp of Kingswood Cottages. He enlisted in May 1915 in the 2nd Bucks and crossed to France as a Corporal. He was killed on 19 July 1916 in an attack on German lines near Laventie. He was a most conscientious and capable N.C.O. and was in Captain Church's Company.

BERESFORD EDGAR SYDNEY. – The only son of Edgar and Alice Sydney of 'The Cock and Rabbit', The-Lee. He enlisted in September 1914 in the 2/12 London, and during his military career saw service in Malta, Egypt, Gallipoli and France. He was killed by the side of his officer (who wrote of him as a splendidly brave and reliable soldier) at Albert on 11 August 1918. He was in his 29th year.

CHARLES TALMER. – The fourth son of Alfred and Emma Talmer of Lee Common. He enlisted in August 1915 in the Machine Gun Corps. He was wounded in the thigh and died from his wounds on 24 September 1916 in hospital at Manchester. He lies buried in The-Lee Churchyard.

HARRY TALMER. – The third son of Alfred and Emma Talmer of Lee Common. He enlisted in November 1914 in the 1st Bucks Battalion and was killed at Pozières during the Battle of the Somme on 21 July 1916.

ROWLAND HENRY WOOD. – The husband of Jeanie Wood and the only son of Captain and Adjt. John Wood. He was a 2nd Lieutenant in the 15th Middlesex Regiment and died from appendicitis on 4 July 1917.

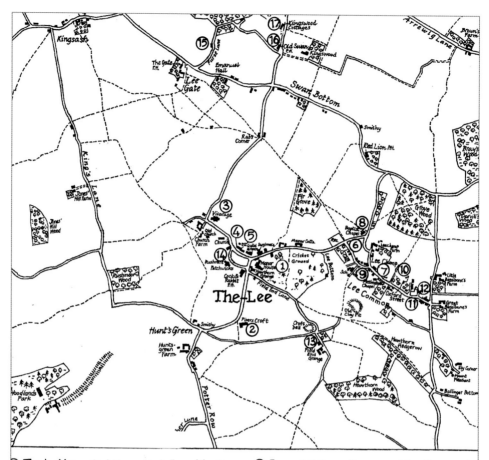

① **The-Lee Manor**: Sir Arthur and Lady Emma Liberty.
② **Pipers Croft**: Ivor and Evelyn, (née Phipps), Stewart-Liberty.
③ **The Vicarage**: Canon Constantine and Mabel Phipps and their children Joan, Jim and Charles†.
④ **The Old Cottage**: Harry Jacobs, estate manager for Sir Arthur Liberty.
⑤ **The-Lee Post Office**: Postmistress Miss Charlotte Stone.
⑥ **Rodwells**: Ernest Young, headmaster of Lee Common School.
⑦ **Laurel Villa**, (now Laurel House), : "Holy" Jim Pearce and his wife Sarah with eight children.
⑧ **The Baptist Chapel**: now private homes belonging to members of the Pearce family. The tombstones of "Holy" Jim Pearce, Dora and Joe Pratt are in the front garden.

⑨ **Prospect Cottage**: George and Ellen Pratt with five children including Joe and Harry †.
⑩ **Crocketts, Crocketts Lane**: Sydney Dwight †, one of four sons of Jesse and Lydia Dwight.
⑪ **Lee Common Post Office** (now Floral Cottage): Mr. and Mrs. George Lewington.
⑫ **Ivy Cottage**, (now Milton): Harry and Leah Brown and four sons including Ralph† and Arthur †.
⑬ **Field End Cottage**: Arnold Morris † with his wife Emily and three children.
⑭ **Rushmere**: Ashley "Budgie" Cummins and wife Mary
⑮ **Furze Field Lane**: Harry Harding†, son of Thomas and Amelia Harding.
⑯ **The Old Swan P.H.**: Percy Price†, son of Albert Price.
⑰ **Kingswood Cottages**: Edward Sharp†, son of Alfred and Jane Sharp.
† *Killed at Fromelles 1916.*

Where the main characters lived in 1914.

APPENDIX B

A TOUR OF THE
FROMELLES BATTLEFIELD

The following itinerary covers the main points of interest in the Fromelles area. It includes the memorials, cemeteries and key geographical features associated with the attack. This tour – by car and on foot – will take about half a day. The Michelin Tourist Map 51, overprinted with the Commonwealth War Cemeteries and Memorials, is very useful.

Start in Fromelles, which is on the D141 between Aubers and Le Maisnil. Next to the *mairie* is a square dedicated to the Battle of Fromelles (1). The commemoration plaque is fixed to the brick wall that encloses one side of the square. While in Fromelles, visit the church. Note the carved wooden crucifix behind the altar. In 1916 the church tower was fortified and used as a German observation post. At this point, the ground is some 60 feet above the flat, low-lying battle area, giving the Germans a clear view of the British and Australian front line and communication trenches.

From Fromelles take the D22 (which becomes the D22c) signed towards Laventie. The northern flank of the attack – from Cardonnerie Farm (which still exists) to Delangre Farm (now a ruin) – is on your right running almost parallel with the D22c. The 8th Australian Brigade attacked across this area and reached a point near Delangre Farm (2).

Head towards Le Trou and Rue Delvas passing on your right a crucifix dedicated to Capt Paul Kennedy and three of his friends in the Rifle Brigade who were killed on 9 May 1915 during the attack on Aubers Ridge (3). The original carving of Christ, which was erected in 1921 by Lady Kennedy, is now in Fromelles church and a replacement crucifix has been placed under the canopy.

Some 300 yards from the crucifix towards Le Trou is the Australian Memorial Park (4). The Memorial Park contains the remains of German

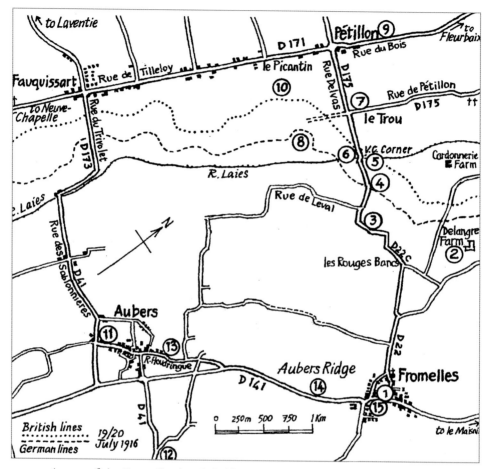

A tour of the Fromelles battlefield.

blockhouses and is on the German front line. This section of the German line was captured and held for several hours by the Australian 14th Brigade during the night of 19/20 July 1916. In the Memorial Park is a most impressive bronze sculpure, *Cobbers*, showing 3101 Sgt Simon Fraser of the 57th Battalion rescuing a wounded soldier of the 60th Battalion. The sculpture is the work of Peter Corlett of Melbourne and was unveiled in July 1998 when the park was dedicated. At the entrance to the park are some useful information panels.

Two hundred yards further along Rue Delvas is VC Corner Cemetery (5). This is the only all-Australian cemetery in France. On the screen wall, behind the Cross of Sacrifice, are the names of 1,298 Australians who died in the Fromelles attack and have no known graves. In the garden are the remains of 410 unidentified Australians. A remembrance service takes place here on 19 July each year.

Continue along Rue Delvas towards Le Trou and cross the River Laies (also spelt 'Layes') (6). In 1916 this part of the Laies was in No-Man's-Land. Today, as then, it is little more than a drainage ditch.

Le Trou (7) was the site of the Australian 15th Brigade Headquarters and nearby was a first aid post. The Le Trou Aid Post Cemetery is reached by a small footbridge over a moat. It contains 351 graves, 56 Australian and the remainder British. The unidentified British and Australian graves are all probably from 19–20 July.

Off Rue Delvas in Le Trou, in line with Rue Petillon (D175), is a track bordered on one side by tall trees. Walk 700 yards along the line of the track from its junction with Rue Delvas and you will be in the middle of No-Man's-Land between the British lines and the German strongpoint, the Sugar Loaf (8). Note the flatness of the attack area. It was across this ground that the 2/1st Bucks, including the men from The Lee, made their assault. Many British and Australian troops lost their lives in front of the Sugar Loaf.

At the crossroads in Petillon turn right along the D171 towards Fleurbaix and stop at the Rue du Bois Cemetery (9). In this cemetery, Plot I (Row B) and Plot II (Row A) contain men from the 2/1st Bucks and the 15th Australian Brigade killed at Fromelles. Maj G.C. McCrae, the CO of the Australian 60th Battalion, is buried here.

Return through Petillon along Rue du Tilleloy (D171). This stretch of Rue du Tilleloy, immediately after the junction with Rue Delvas, runs roughly parallel with the British front line, which was some 500 yards on the left. The 2/1st Bucks trenches were at this point (10). British artillery observation posts were sited in the ruined houses along Rue du Tilleloy and many of the observers died as a result of the accurate German shelling from Aubers Ridge.

Continue along the D171 to Fauquissart and turn left into the D173 (Rue du Trivolet) towards Aubers. This road marks the extreme southern flank of the Fromelles attack. The 2/7th Warwicks had early success here on the evening of 19 July. Cross the River Laies which at this point was behind the German lines. Follow Rue des Sablonnieres into Aubers. Note how the ground steadily rises. In Aubers, in Rue Basse, are the remains of a German fortified observation post (11).

In Aubers visit the Aubers Ridge Cemetery (12). Of the 718 graves, 441 have no name. Plot I has 17 named Australians killed on 19 July and Plot II contains dead of the British 61st Division. Many of these bodies were brought to this cemetery by Germans who held this position in 1916. Before leaving Aubers visit the remains of the German blockhouse in Rue Houdringue (13).

From Aubers take the road towards Fromelles (D141). You are travelling along the Aubers Ridge where the Germans positioned their artillery. Note the commanding view over the attack area. The row of trees off Rue Delvas (see 8) is clearly visible.

Just before Fromelles is a German third-line concrete bunker. The upper floor was used as an artillery observation post and the lower floor sheltered soldiers (14).

In Fromelles visit the fascinating museum (15) which occupies the top floor of the mairie. The museum contains an amazing collection of artefacts – Australian, British and German – connected with the attack at Fromelles. The Museum is run by the local Association pour le Souvenir de la Bataille de Fromelles (ASBF).

* * *

ADDITIONAL TOURS

There are four other areas connected with the Fromelles attack that are worth visiting.

For visitors travelling along the A26 from Calais to the Fromelles area there is the opportunity to follow the route marched by the 2/1st Bucks soon after they had arrived in France in May 1916. The Battalion detrained from Le Havre at Berguette, near Isbergues, and took the route St-Venant, Le Sart, Merville, Estaires, Laventie. In the Communal Cemetery at Merville (on the D38 to Neuf-Berquin) are the graves of Ralph Brown (XIB36) and Harry Pratt (VB8) from The Lee. The grave of Harold Church, also in the 2/1st Bucks, can be found in the Laventie Military Cemetery (XIB36), La Gorgue, just north of Laventie.

In Laventie, on the wall of the *mairie*, next to the church, is a plaque dedicated to the British 61st Division which spent most of the war in that area. The plaque was erected in 1935 and has on it all the cap-badges of the battalions who made up the Division, including that of the 2/1st Bucks. The plaque is inscribed: 'The Division first served during the Great War in the neighbourhood of this town of Laventie and is proud to leave its dead sleeping in the sacred soil of France.'

Adolf Hitler was billeted during his time near Fromelles at 1,345 Rue Faidherbe, Fournes-en-Weppe. Fournes is about 3 miles east of Fromelles along the D141A. The commemorative plaque that was erected on the wall of this house by the Germans in 1942 is now in the museum in Fromelles.

At Loos-en-Gohelle, about 3 miles north-west of Lens on the N43, is the Loos Memorial, part of Dud Corner Cemetery. The memorial commemorates over 20,000 officers and men who died in the area of the River Lys and who have no known grave. Panels 83–5 have inscribed on them the names of seven men from The Lee who were killed at Fromelles.

NOTES AND REFERENCES

Chapter One

1. G.D. Roberts, *Without My Wig* (Macmillan & Co. Ltd, 1957).
2. *Bucks Examiner*, 24 July 1914.
3. From a transcription of a signed presentation, 1913, in possession of Mrs A.I. Stewart-Liberty.
4. *The Lee Magazine*, July 1914.
5. *Ibid.*, December 1913.
6. *Ibid.*, June 1920.
7. *Bucks Examiner*, 24 July 1914.
8. St John the Baptist church, The Lee, registers of baptisms and marriages.
9. Alison Adburgham, *Liberty's: A Biography of a Store* (Unwin Hyman, 1975), ch. X.
10. *The Lee Magazine*, July 1914.
11. Arthur Liberty published a pamphlet, *The Doings in The Parish During Coronation Month*, in July 1911. In this document he records the various festivities in The Lee and takes the opportunity to outline the story of the parish boundary changes and the extension of the church. He notes that the ecclesiastical boundaries of the parish were extended in 1896.
12. *Ibid.*
13. *Ibid.*
14. Adburgham, *Liberty's*.
15. *Statistics of the Military Effort of the British Empire during the Great War* (HMSO, 1922). Owing to incomplete statistical records in some countries, accurate casualty figures will never be known. The total number of dead of all the belligerents is estimated to be 10–13 million.
16. M. Eksteins, *Rites of Spring* (Papermac, 1989), p. 130.
17. *Bucks Examiner*, 23 January 1914.
18. The Lee Parish Minute Book, 1914.
19. *Bucks Herald*, 8 August 1914.
20. Included in the Oxford Book of War Poetry, ed. Jon Stallworthy (Oxford University Press, 1984) 'MCMXIV'.

Chapter Two

1. Niall Ferguson, in *The Pity of War* (Penguin, 1998), p. 67, argues that the geographical position of Belgium (and the Netherlands) necessitated Britain's control over them so that effective economic pressure could be applied to Germany. 'In other words, if Germany had not violated Belgium's neutrality in 1914, Britain would have.'
2. *The Lee Magazine*, September 1914.
3. Quotations in this and the preceding paragraph are from *The Lee Magazine*, September and October 1914.
4. K. Robbins, *The First World War* (OUP, 1984), p. 19.
5. Ferguson, *The Pity of War*, p. 319.
6. B. Tuchman, *August 1914* (Constable, 1962), p. 123.

7. Philip Magnus, *Kitchener* (Penguin, 1968), p. 339.
8. *The Lee Magazine*, October 1914.
9. *Bucks Examiner*, 23 October 1914.
10. *Bucks Herald*, 17 October 1914.
11. *Ibid.*, 24 October 1914.
12. Roberts, *Without My Wig*, p. 96.
13. *Bucks Herald*, 17 October 1914.
14. *The Lee Magazine*, October 1914.
15. *Ibid.*, October 1914.
16. The Chancellor of the Exchequer, David Lloyd George, had announced on 4 August 1914 that the Government 'would enable the trades of this country to carry out business as usual'. Professor Ian Beckett, *The Great War 1914–1918* (Longman, 2001), p. 46.
17. *The Lee Magazine*, June 1915.
18. *Ibid.*, July 1916.
19. *Ibid.*, February 1915.
20. *Ibid.*
21. *Ibid.*, March 1915.
22. *Ibid.*, July 1915
23. *Ibid.*, June 1916.
24. Magnus, *Kitchener*, p. 345.
25. *The Lee Magazine*, January 1915.
26. *Ibid.*, March 1915.
27. *Ibid.*, September 1915.
28. *Ibid.*, October 1914.
29. *Ibid.*, January 1915.
30. *Bucks Herald*, 7 November 1914.
31. *The Lee Magazine*, March 1915.
32. *Bucks Examiner*, 21 August 1914.
33. *The Lee Magazine*, April 1915.
34. *Ibid.*, January 1915.
35. *Ibid.*, July 1916.
36. *Bucks Examiner*, 7 July 1916.
37. *Ibid.*, 16 August 1916.
38. *The Lee Magazine*, June 1915.

Chapter Three

1. Beckett, *The Great War*, p. 210.
2. Martin Middlebrook, in his *Your Country Needs You* (Leo Cooper, Pen and Sword Books, 2000), describes how the British Army expanded during the war.
3. The battalions of a regiment were generally spread among different brigades. Once 'brigaded' a battalion remained in that brigade. A division was a self-contained fighting unit made up of three brigades. In addition to infantry brigades, it included: artillery, cavalry, engineers, medical, military police, ordnance, postal services and veterinary support units. Divisions usually remained intact, but were frequently transferred between corps and armies. The structure of an army, together with the ranks of the commanders of the various units, was broadly:

Unit	Rank	Approx. nos
Infantry Section	NCO	10
Platoon	2 Lt	50
Company	Capt (2i/c Lt)	220
Battalion	Lt Col (2i/c Maj)	1,000
Brigade	Brig Gen	5,000
Division	Maj Gen	15,000
Corps	Lt Gen	36,000
Army	Gen	180,000

4. *Bucks Examiner*, 7 August 1914.
5. *Bucks Herald*, 8 August 1914.
6. Letter from Tonman Mosely, Chairman, the Bucks TFA in *The Bucks Herald*, 10 October 1914.
7. Lt Col G. Christie-Miller DSO, MC, *The Second Bucks Battalion 1914–18: An Unofficial Record*, 2 vols. Unless otherwise stated, quotations in this chapter referring to the formation and training of the 2/1 Bucks Battalion come from these typed volumes which are kept in the Aylesbury Reference Library.

8. Professor Ian Beckett in *The Call To Arms* (Barracuda Books, 1985) points out (p. 73) that 'it was a matter of Territorial Association Policy that no pressure should be applied to recruits to join either the Territorials or the Regulars when they presented themselves at recruiting offices. As a result, by 20 June 1915, the Association had found 3,291 men for the Territorials and 2,640 for the New Armies.'

9. Maj Gen J.C. Swann, *Citizen Soldiers of Bucks* (Aylesbury: Bucks TA Association, 1930), p. 133

10. Charles Phipps's pocket diary and letters are kept in the Centre for Buckinghamshire Studies, Aylesbury, DX/780.

11. *The Lee Magazine*, September 1915.

12. Swann, *Citizen Soldiers*, p. 136.

13. *Bucks Herald*, 24 June 1916.

14. Letter in possession of Mrs Joy Peace, daughter of Joe Pratt.

15. 'I'll Make a Man of You' from the revue, *The Passing Show*, words by Arthur Wimperis and music by Herman Fink.

16. From the papers of Lt Col G. Christie-Miller held in the Imperial War Museum, IWM 80/32/1.

17. *The Lee Magazine*, June 1916.

18. Typewritten sheet by Ivor Stewart-Liberty headed *Memoirs of a New Battalion in 1914*. Held in the Centre for Buckinghamshire Studies, Aylesbury, DX/780.

Chapter Four

1. A.J.P. Taylor, *The First World War* (Penguin, 1996), p. 34.

2. A.J.P. Taylor, *English History 1914–1945* (OUP, 1965), p. 12.

3. The letters and diary of Charles Phipps are held in the Centre for Buckinghamshire Studies, Aylesbury, DX/780.

4. The 182nd Brigade wore squares; the 183rd wore triangles and the 184th circles. The battalions were identified by wearing their brigade markings in different colours according to seniority: red for the senior battalion then blue, yellow and black.

5. G.D. Roberts's letter is held in the Westminster City Archives, 788/169 (9).

6. Lt Col G. Christie-Miller DSO, MC, *The Second Bucks Battalion 1914–18: An Unofficial Record*, 2 vols. Unless otherwise stated, quotations in this chapter referring to the formation and training of the 2/1 Bucks Battalion come from these typed volumes which are kept in the Aylesbury Reference Library.

7. On 5 June 1916, Kitchener was drowned when HMS *Hampshire* struck a mine north of Scotland en route for Russia.

8. A communication trench linking the front line with Laventie.

9. Christie-Miller papers in the Imperial War Museum, IWM 80/32/2.

10. Westminster City Archives, 788/169 (9).

11. Ivor Stewart-Liberty's and Charles Phipps's letters are held in the Centre for Buckinghamshire Studies, Aylesbury, DX/780.

12. Roberts, *Without My Wig*.

13. Christie-Miller, *The Second Bucks Battalion*. Unless otherwise stated, quotations and anecdotes in this chapter are from this record.

Chapter Five

1. Ivor Stewart-Liberty letters are held in the Centre For Buckinghamshire Studies, Aylesbury, DX/780.
2. Extract from Haig's Diary quoted in Duff Cooper, *Haig* (Faber and Faber, 1935), vol. I, p. 317.
3. Correlli Barnett, *The Great War* (Classic Penguin, 2000), p. 75.
4. Quotations in this paragraph are from the *British Official History of The Great War: Military Operations, vol. II: France and Belgium, 1916,* compiled by Capt Wilfrid Miles (Imperial War Museum and The Battery Press, 1992), p. 119. Abbreviated to BOH.
5. C.E.W. Bean, *A.I.F. in France, Vol. III*, p. 322. Abbreviated to AOH.
6. First Army Report on Fromelles, Australian War Museum 252 (A184). Abbreviated to AWM.
7. The boundaries of the two opposing forces did not coincide exactly, but, broadly, the 8th and 14th Australian Brigades were faced by the 21st Bavarian Reserve Regiment; the 15th Australian and the 184th and 183rd British Brigades by the 16th Bavarian Reserve Regiment; and the 182nd British Brigade by the 17th Bavarian Reserve Regiment.
8. BOH, p. 121.
9. *Ibid.*
10. BOH, p. 123.
11. AWM, p. 252.
12. *Ibid.*
13. AOH, p. 347.
14. AWM, p. 252.
15. AOH, p. 348.
16. BOH, p. 125.
17. *Ibid.*
18. Public Records Office (PRO), ref. WO 9513066.
19. Christie-Miller, *The Second Bucks Battalion*, p. 183.
20. AOH, p. 339.
21. *The Lee Magazine*, Sept. 1916.
22. Dr Fridolin Solleder, *Vier Jahre Westfront: Geschichte des Regiments List R.J.R. 16* (Munchen: Verlag Max Schick, 1932), p. 214.
23. Article in the *North German Gazette*, 3 August 1916.
24. BOH, p.126.
25. Christie-Miller, *The Second Bucks Battalion*, p. 180.
26. BOH, p. 126, footnote (2).
27. Christie-Miller, *Second Bucks Battalion*, p. 184.
28. *Ibid.*, p. 179.
29. The pocket diary of Pte Penny is held at the Imperial War Museum, IWM 88/52/11.
30. The pocket diary of Spr Hollwey is held at the Imperial War Museum, IWM 98/17/1.
31. AOH, p. 355, note 38.
32. Public Records Office (PRO), WO 95/3066.
33. BOH, p. 124, footnote (1).
34. Christie-Miller, *Second Bucks Battalion*, p. 184.
35. The accounts of these events by Charles Phipps and Ivor Stewart-Liberty do not correspond exactly with that of the 2/1st Bucks War Diary (PRO WO 95/3066). The probable sequence seems to have been: D and C Companies went into billets on 17 July. C Company returned to the trenches on 18 July when A Company was gassed. A Company then went into billets with D Company leaving C Company in the front line. A and D Companies joined C Company in the trenches on the morning of 19 July.

36. *The Lee Magazine*, October 1916.
37. Charles Phipps's diary is held at the Centre for Buckinghamshire Studies, Aylesbury, DX/780.

Chapter Six

1. *The Lee Magazine*, October 1916.
2. Quoted in Solleder, *Vier Jahre Westfront*, p. 215.
3. *The Lee Magazine*, October 1916.
4. PRO WO95/3066.
5. The pocket diary of Spr Hollwey is held at the Imperial War Museum, IWM 98/17/1.
6. *The Lee Magazine*, October 1916.
7. BOH, p. 128.
8. AOH, p. 391, refers to 'the gallant Captain Church'.
9. Christie-Miller, *Second Bucks Battalion*, p. 145.
10. *The South Bucks Free Press*, 20 October 1916.
11. From 'The Silent One', included in *The Oxford Book of War Poetry*, ed. Jon Stallworthy (OUP), 1984.
12. ANZAC refers to the area – ANZAC Cove – fought over by the Australian troops in Gallipoli.
13. AOH, p. 392.
14. *Ibid.*, p. 394.
15. Solleder, *Vier Jahre Westfront*, p. 222.
16. 2/1st Bucks Battalion War Diary, PRO, WO 95/3066.
17. Christie-Miller, *Second Bucks Battalion*, p. 187.
18. E.C. Penny DCM, personal notebook, Imperial War Museum 88/52/11.
19. Quoted in Robin S. Corfield, *Don't Forget Me Cobber* (Corfield & Co., Victoria, Australia, 2000), p. 172.
20. Quoted in Corfield, p. 229.
21. F.W.D. Lockwood CBE, personal diary, Imperial War Museum 90/21/1.

22. 2/1st Bucks War Diary, Appendix D.
23. *Ibid.*
24. *Ibid.*
25. *Ibid.*
26. Australian War Memorial Archives, 1/22/4.
27. 2/1st Bucks War Diary.
28. BOH, note on p. 135.
29. Christie-Miller, *Second Bucks Battalion*, p. 173.
30. BOH, p. 134.
31. AOH, p. 444.
32. PRO CAB 45/134.
33. PRO CAB 45/136.
34. Article in *Duckboard*, 1 September 1930, AWM Archives 4-14934.
35. Christie-Miller, *Second Bucks Battalion*, p. 191.
36. AOH, p. 447.
37. *Duckboard*.
38. PRO CAB 45/138.
39. PRO CAB 45/134.
40. Corfield, p. 272.
41. Lt Col A.F. Mockler-Ferryman, *The Oxfordshire and Buckinghamshire Light Infantry Chronicle 1916–1917* (Eyre & Spottiswood), vol. xxvi, p. 270.
42. *The Lee Magazine*, January 1921.

Chapter Seven

1. The Phippses' letters are held in the Centre for Buckinghamshire Studies, Aylesbury, DX/780.
2. Published in *The Bucks Free Press*, 11 August 1916.
3. *Bucks Examiner*, 28 July 1916.
4. *Bucks Herald*, 29 July 1916.
5. Roberts, *Without My Wig*, p. 169.
6. The Phippses' letters.
7. The Loos Memorial is in Pas de Calais near Loos-en-Gohelle about 4 miles north-west of Lens. The names of The Lee men are on panels 83–5.

8. Merville Communal Cemetery, Nord. Merville is 10 miles north of Béthune. The grave references are VB8 (Harry Pratt) and XIB36 (Ralph Brown). Although Harry Pratt was killed some days before the attack at Fromelles, the tradition in The Lee has been to include his name among those who were killed on 19 July. In this book that tradition has been preserved.

9. *The Lee Magazine*, January 1916.

10. James Thomas Pearce of Swan Bottom joined the 2nd Battalion Ox and Bucks LI in September 1914. He was reported missing after the Battle of Festubert 1915 and concluded killed 16 May 1915. *The Lee Magazine* of January 1921 lists the particulars of the thirty men from The Lee who were killed in the First World War and these are shown in Appendix A.

11. *The Lee Magazine*, September 1916.

12. *Ibid.*, July 1917.

13. *Ibid.*, January 1918.

14. *Ibid.*, June 1917.

15. *Ibid.*, September 1917.

16. *Ibid.*, May 1919.

17. *Ibid.*, June 1919.

18. Roberts, *Without My Wig*.

19. Joseph E. Parsico, *Nuremberg* (Penguin, 1995), p. 348.

20. Beckett in *The Call To Arms* points out that, in 1916, 68 per cent of the 2/1st Bucks dead were from Buckinghamshire parishes while, in 1917, the proportion had reduced to 43 per cent.

21. Lt Col Spencer's papers are held in the Imperial War Museum, IWM 87/26/1.

22. War Office 35/Gen No 1827 (AG2a).

23. In 1920, Ivor Stewart-Liberty gave land to both Great Missenden and Ballinger for the purpose of erecting war memorials.

24. The main cemeteries in which the British and Australian dead of the Fromelles attack are buried are: Aubers Ridge British Cemetery; Le Trou Aid Post Cemetery; Rue du Bois Cemetery; Laventie Military Cemetery (La Gorgue) – where Harold Church is buried; the Merville Communal Cemetery; the Loos Memorial; and VC Corner Cemetery. German dead are buried at the Fournes, Beaucamps and Wicres Cemeteries.

25. VC Corner took its name from a communication trench of that name that ran back from the front at that point. Up to the time of the Fromelles attack, twenty-nine VCs had been awarded for acts of bravery in that area (Festubert–Neuve Chapelle–Fromelles–Armentières) and six more were to be awarded by the end of the war. See Corfield p. 357.

26. Sculpted by Peter Corlett of Melbourne and unveiled 5 July 1998.

27. Ralph Rodwell of Lee Common served with the 9th Battalion Ox and Bucks and died of meningitis in December 1916. Charles Talmer, also of Lee Common, was in the Machine Gun Corps. He was wounded and invalided back to England where he died in September 1916.

28. *The Lee Magazine*, February 1918.

SELECT BIBLIOGRAPHY

PUBLISHED MATERIAL

Adburgham, Alison, *Liberty's, A Biography of a Store*, Unwin Hyman, 1975

Arthur, Max, *When This Bloody War Is Over*, Piatkus, 2001

Ascoli, David, *The Mons Star*, Birlinn, 2001

Ashworth, Tony, *Trench Warfare 1914–1918: The Live and Let Live System*, Pan, 1980

Barnett, Correlli, *The Great War*, Classic Penguin, 2000

Bean, C.E.W., *Official History of Australia in the Great War 1914–18*, Angus and Robertson, 1942

Beckett, I.F.W., *The Call To Arms*, Barracuda Books Ltd, 1985

——, *The Amateur Military Tradition: 1558–1945*, Manchester University Press, 1991

——, *The Great War 1914–18*, Longmans, 2001

Bishop, James, *London Illustrated News Social History of the First World War*, Angus and Robertson, 1982

Bond, Brian *et al*, *Look to Your Front*, Spellmount, 1999

Borman, Derek, *At the Going Down of the Sun*, Borman, Dunnington Hall, York, 1988

Brown, Malcolm, *The Imperial War Museum Book of the Western Front*, Pan Books, 2001

Cooper, Duff, *Haig*, vols 1 and 2, Faber and Faber, 1935

Corfield, Robin S., *Don't Forget Me Cobber*, Corfield & Co., Victoria, Australia, 2000

Crutwell, C.R.M.F., *A History of the Great War 1914–1918*, Oxford University Press, 1934

Eksteins, M., *Rites of Spring*, Papermac, 1989

Ferguson, Niall, *The Pity of War*, Penguin, 1998

Gilbert, Martin, *First World War*, Weidenfeld and Nicolson, 1994

Haswell, Jock, *The British Army*, Thames and Hudson, 1980

Haythornthwaite, Philip J., *The World War One Source Book*, Arms and Armour, 1992

Johnson, J.H., *Stalemate*, Cassell Military Classics, 1995

Keegan, John, *The First World War*, Hutchinson, 1998

Lloyd, T.O., *Empire to Welfare State: English History 1906–85*, Oxford University Press, 1991

Macdonald, Lyn, *Somme*, Papermac, 1983

——, *1914*, Penguin, 1989

Magnus, Philip, *Kitchener*, Penguin, 1968

Middlebrook, Martin, *The First Day of The Somme*, Penguin, 1984

——, *Your Country Needs You*, Leo Cooper, Pen and Sword, 2000

Miles, Capt Wilfrid, *British Official History of the Great War. Military Operations France and Belgium 1916*, vol ii, Imperial War Museum and the Battery Press, 1992

Mockler-Ferryman, Lt Col A.F., *The Oxfordshire and Buckinghamshire Light Infantry Chronicle 1916–17*, vol xxvi, Eyre and Spottiswood, *c.* 1920s

Newbolt, Sir Henry, *The Story of The Oxfordshire and Buckinghamshire Light Infantry*, County Life Library, 1915

Parsico, Joseph E., *Nuremberg*, Penguin, 1995

Priestley, J.B., *The Edwardians*, Sphere Books Ltd, 1970

Robbins, Keith, *The First World War*, Oxford University Press, 1985

Roberts, G.D., *Without My Wig*, Macmillan & Co. Ltd, 1957

Sellwood, A.V., *The Saturday Night Soldiers*, Wolfe Publishing Ltd, 1966

Solleder, Dr Fridolin, *Vier Jahre Westfront: Geschichte des Regiments List R.J.R.16*, Verlag Max Schick, Munich, 1932

Stallworthy, Jon (ed.), *The Oxford Book of War Poetry*, Oxford University Press, 1984

Strachan, Hew, *The First World War*, vol. i, Oxford University Press, 2001

Swann, Maj Gen J.C., *Citizen Soldiers of Buckinghamshire 1795–1926*, Buckinghamshire Territorial Army Association, 1930

Taylor, A.J.P., *English History 1914–1945*, Oxford University Press, 1965

——, *The First World War*, Penguin, 1966

Terraine, John, *Douglas Haig, The Educated Soldier*, Leo Cooper, 1990

——, *The Great War*, Wordsworth Military Library, 1998

Trevelyan, G.M., *Grey of Falloden*, Longmans, 1937

Tuchman, Barbara, *August 1914*, Constable, 1962

Warner, Philip, *Field Marshal Earl Haig*, Cassell Military Paperbacks, 1991

Westlake, Ray, *Kitchener's Army*, Spellmount, 1998

Winter, Jay, *Sites of Memory, Sites of Mourning*, Cambridge University Press, 1997

——, *The Experience of World War One*, Grange Books, 1988

Unpublished Material

The Centre for Buckinghamshire Studies

Christie-Miller, Lt Col G., *The Second Bucks Battalion 1914–18. An Unofficial Record*, 2 vols

Stewart-Liberty, I., Letters, 1914–16, DX 780

Phipps, Charles and James, letters and diary, 1914–16, DX 780

The Lee Magazine, 1914–1926 (incomplete set)

Published Material

Bucks Advertiser, Bucks Examiner, Bucks Herald, 1914–16, *South Bucks Free Press*, 1916.

Westminster City Archives

Roberts, G.D., Letters. 788/168(9)

SELECT BIBLIOGRAPHY

THE IMPERIAL WAR MUSEUM

Christie-Miller, G., Papers, IWM 80/32/2
Penny, E.C., Notebook, IWM 88/52/11
Hollwey, W.H., Diary, IWM 98/17/1
Lockwood, F.W.D., Diary, 90/21/1
Spencer, A.V. Letter, 87/26/1

LEE COMMON FIRST SCHOOL

School Log Book, 1909–49
School Managers' Minute Book, 1913–21

INDEX

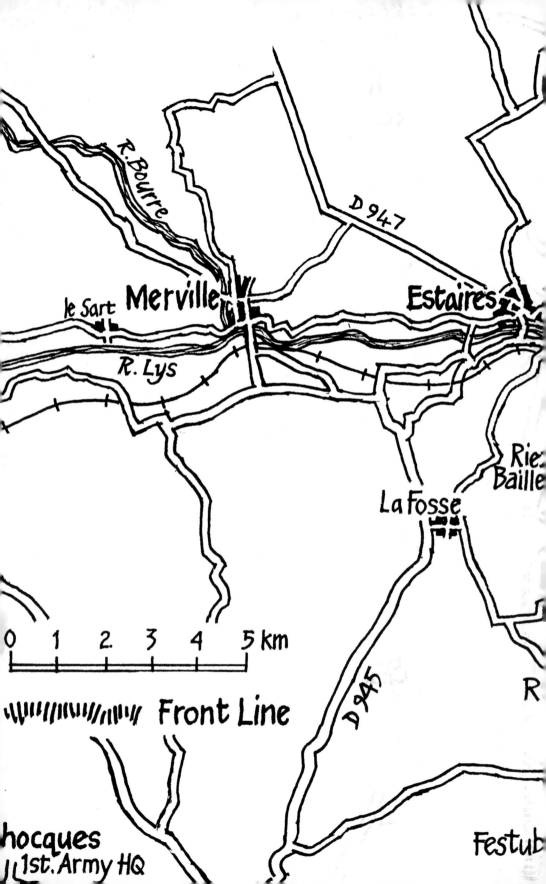

R. Bourre

D 947

le Sart   **Merville**   **Estaires**

R. Lys

Rie.
Baille

La Fosse

0 1 2 3 4 5 km

〰〰〰 Front Line

D 945

R

hocques
1st. Army HQ

Festub